WordPress SEO 2017

Optimize Your WordPress Site for Better Rankings!

By Dr. Andy Williams

ezSEONews.com

Version 1.0
Updated: 1st March 2017

What People Have Said About Versions of This Book

The original version of this book was published in 2013. This edition brings the subject of Wordpress SEO right up to date. The book has had major re-edits and all new sections. Some sections have even been removed altogether as no longer relevant.

The following comments are from customers over this timespan and may refer to any one of the major versions released since 2012.

"Very good book not only for Wordpress SEO but any site SEO - explains the concepts behind tweaking your site I learned a lot from this book - it is now my guide to the world of SEO" **Gfergy**

"If you are using, or intend to use, WordPress as your website development platform, you NEED to read this book if you want to maximize your organic traffic.

I've been following Dr. Andy's work for the last decade or so and have always structured my websites along the principles he describes and I'm happy to report that they've sold a tad over £9M since 2003 (That's not the same as profit Mr. HMRC) based at least partly on organic traffic." **Pete Bennett**

"I am a huge fan of Dr. Andy's writing and have virtually all his books. The two reasons for this are a) he puts in the research time and has excellent analytical skills and b) he can put technical points across in a way that even a non-technical person such as me can understand.

This book is no exception to the rule. If you run a Wordpress blog and you want to get visitors, this book is a no-brainer." ***Pearson Brown***

"This book has plenty of screen shots showing very clearly what to do. It is not excessively technical like many internet books. This is important because every business person needs a website but most of us have neither time nor inclination to become IT experts, that time would be better spent on perfecting our own trade or profession." **Aquilonian**

"Just what a near-Luddite like me needs to hold my hand through refining my WordPress website. I definitely recommend this book for you non-techies out there." ***Mike R***

"This is a fantastic step by step guide, very easy to follow even for people who know nothing about SEO!! Thanks for putting together such a great guide I will be reading some more of your books in the near future!" *Amazon Customer*

"I've been running Wordpress websites for years and never taken my site speed seriously. Thanks for Dr. Williams advice my site speed profile has rocketed. I've learnt a great deal about how to make the most from Cache and SEO plugins." **Matt Smith**

Contents

Introduction..1

1. The Biggest Sin – Duplicate Content 2

2. WordPress Web Hosting... 4

   2.1. CDN (Content Delivery Network)................................5

   2.2. Shared Hosting & Dedicated Servers 5

3. Themes & Theme Settings 10

4. Google Tools 14

   4.1 Google Search Console 14

   4.2 Google Analytics 15

   4.3 Google's Webmaster Guidelines 16

5. Screen Options 17

6. WordPress Settings Menu 19

   6.1. General Settings 19

   6.2. Writing Settings 20

   6.3. Reading Settings 20

   6.4 Discussion Settings 23

   6.5. Media Settings..28

   6.6 Permalinks Settings 28

7. Plugins 31

   7.1. Essential Plugins 31

     1. Yoast SEO 31

     2. W3 Total Cache...32

     3. Dynamic Widgets...32

   7.2 Non-essential Plugins 33

     1. YARPP 33

     2. Contact form 7 34

     3. UpdraftPlus..34

4. Broken Link Checker...35

5. Social Media Flying Icons...36

6. Stop Spammers Spam Prevention..36

7. Pretty Link Lite..37

8. All in One Security & Firewall...38

9. CI Backlinks 38

8. Keeping WordPress Up to Date - WordPress & Plugins 39

9. Duplication on Category, Tag & Other Archive Pages 41

10. Menus & Site Navigation 46

   10.1. Recommended Navigation...48

   10.2. Implementing the Four Main Navigation Features................49

      10.2.1. Implementing Legal Menus 49

      10.2.2. Implementing a Search Box 54

      10.2.3. Main Site Navigation Menu 55

      10.2.4. Dynamic Navigation Menus 55

11. Comment System.. 62

12. RSS Feeds 63

13. Google Authorship & WordPress User Profiles........................ 66

   13.1. Google Authorship 66

   13.2. Gravatars & the Author Bio on Your Site.........................67

      13.2.1. Author Bio Boxes...68

14. Robots.txt File 71

15. WWW or No WWW?.. 72

16. Pages Versus Posts 74

   16.1. Posts..74

   16.2. Pages...75

   16.3. When to Use WordPress Pages and WordPress Posts............75

17. Setting up the Homepage 77

18. Site-Wide Considerations 80

18.1. "Nofollow" Links 80

18.2. Getting Social on Your Site 80

19. SEO When Writing Content 81

19.1. SEO for WordPress Pages 82

19.2. SEO for WordPress Posts 85

19.2.1. Post Categories...86

19.2.2. Post Tags 87

19.2.3. Post Formatting 88

19.3. Optimizing Images Used in Posts 89

19.4. Internal Linking Between Posts 92

19.5. Featured Images for Posts 93

19.6. Post Excerpts 94

19.7. Allow Comments & Trackbacks on Posts? 95

19.8. Scheduling Posts..96

19.9. A Checklist for Good SEO Content................................97

19.9.1. Titles...97

19.9.2. Headings...98

19.9.3. Theme Your Content 98

19.9.4. Categories & Tags...99

19.9.5. Images 99

19.9.6. Excerpts 100

19.9.7. Linking to Other Content 100

20. Setting up Category Pages 101

20.1. A Category Page Full Post Content............................. 102

20.1.1. Globally Set All Category Pages to Noindex, Follow 103

20.1.2. Setting Individual Category Pages to Noindex, Follow 104

20.2. The Ideal Category Page?... 105

20.3. Formatting the introduction 107

21. Tag Pages 111

22. WordPress SEO Plugin Setup 112

22.1. Dashboard Settings 112

22.2. Title & Metas 121

22.3. Social Settings 131

22.4. XML Sitemap Settings 133

22.4.1. Submitting Your Sitemap(s) to Google 137

22.5. Advanced Settings 138

22.6. Tools 141

22.7. Search Console 141

23. W3 Total Cache Setup 143

23.1. Setting up W3 Total Cache 143

23.1.1. General Settings 144

23.1.2. Page Cache 146

23.1.3. Minify 146

23.1.4. Browser Cache 146

Useful resources 149

Please leave a review on Amazon 150

My other Webmaster books 151

My Video Courses 151

More information from Dr. Andy Williams 151

DISCLAIMER AND TERMS OF USE AGREEMENT

How to Use This Book

This book will take you on a journey that is best followed in the order it is presented. At least for the first time. Once you have been through the entire book, it then works well as a "dip in when you need it" type reference book.

This book is not intended to teach you how to use Wordpress, so you will need a reasonable working knowledge of Wordpress. There are links to my books and courses at the end of this book if you need a refresher course on Wordpress.

A note about UK v US English

There are some differences between UK and US English. While I try to be consistent, some errors may slip into my writing because I spend a lot of time corresponding to people in both the UK and the US. The line can blur.

Examples of this include spelling of words like optimise (UK) v optimize (US).

The difference I get the most complaints about is with collective nouns. Collective nouns refer to a group of individuals, e.g. Google. In the US, collective nouns are singular, so **Google IS** a search engine. However, in the UK, collective nouns are usually plural, so **Google ARE** a search engine.

There are other differences too. I hope that if I have been inconsistent somewhere in this book, it does not detract from the value you get from it.

Typos in this book?

Errors (and inconsistencies previously mentioned) can get through proof-readers, so if you do find any typos or grammatical errors in this book, I'd be very grateful if you could let me know using this email address:

typos@ezseonews.com

Introduction

Search Engine Optimization (SEO), is the process webmasters go through to encourage the search engines to rank their pages higher in the search results. Typically, it involves working on the site itself. This is called on-site SEO, but it also involves working at site promotion, and that is what's known as off-site SEO.

Sites can be built in a number of different ways (PHP, HTML, Flash, etc.), using a wide variety of site-building tools, with common examples being Dreamweaver, Drupal, and WordPress, to name just three. Most websites and blogs share certain features that we can control, and use, to help with the on-site SEO. These features include things like the page title, headlines, body text, ALT tags and so on. In this respect, most sites can be treated in a similar manner when we consider on-site SEO. However, different platforms have their own quirks, and WordPress is no exception. Out-of-the-box WordPress doesn't do itself any SEO favors, and can in fact cause you ranking problems. This book will concentrate specifically for the on-page SEO of WordPress sites, highlighting the problems, and working through the numerous fixes.

By the end of this book, your WordPress site should be well optimized, without being 'over-optimized' (which is itself a contributing factor in Google penalties).

NOTE: This book assumes you are familiar with WordPress. If you are a complete beginner, I would recommend you take the time to learn the basics of Wordpress. At the very end of this book, you'll find links to my other books and video courses. In particular, I have a video course called "Wordpress Essentials" that will get you up to speed fast. If you prefer to read, my Wordpress for Beginners is a comprehensive book to cut the Wordpress learning curve and get you confident and proficient in using Wordpress.

1. The Biggest Sin - Duplicate Content

One of the main considerations when working on a WordPress site is duplicate content. For example, every post you create will also be posted on several other web pages within the site. Whether that post is shown in its entirety on all these pages, or as a shorter 'excerpt', is often controlled by the site's theme. Some themes will let you choose, whereas others will not.

So What Does This Mean to You, the SEO?

When a post is made on a WordPress, it may be published on all of the following web pages on that website, and at the same time:

1. Homepage

2. Post page. Every post is given its own web page.

3. Category page(s). Posts are assigned categories, and the category pages show all posts in that particular category.

4. Date archive page(s). These are pages that show all the posts made on a given date.

5. Tag page(s). Tag pages are another way of organizing your content. You can assign several words or phrases to each post, and for every word or phrase, a tag page is created. These tag pages show all posts that have been tagged with the specific word. Therefore if you used a tag 'blue widget' on five posts, the blue widget tag page will show all five posts.

6. Author page. This is an archive showing all of the posts made by a particular author.

That's six areas where the exact same post may show up!

If you assign just one category to a post, and one tag phrase, that means each post could appear on six web pages of the site **AT THE SAME TIME**. While I recommend you only assign a single post to just one category, tags are different. If you use tags, I'd recommend 3-5 per post. That would take the count up to nine or 10 pages showing identical content.

This type of duplication is bad (very bad!)

So, the general rule that I recommend is to only include the 'full post' on ONE web page of your site. On any other page where that post appears, you should be using excerpts, or in some cases just the title.

Having a high level of control is vital to removing this type of duplication, and the process begins by choosing a good template. The template should allow you to specify what you want to be posted on each of those six areas of potential duplication. I will, therefore, look at themes shortly, and explain what you need to look for when choosing a theme of your own.

First, though, we should mention web hosting.

2. WordPress Web Hosting

OK, so you may be wondering why I am talking about web hosts. After all, isn't this supposed to be a book about WordPress SEO?

Yes, it is. However, the speed at which your site loads (and even the uptime of your site), are factors that are taken into account by search engines. Slow loading websites, or those which are unavailable for long periods of time (because the host server is down), suffer poorer rankings because of it. Sites which go down frequently, negatively impact the reputation you have with your visitors too.

There are many types of web host and lots of different plans that come with each one. You can get shared hosting, a managed or unmanaged Virtual Private Server (VPS), or a Dedicated Server. There are even some hosts that specialize in WordPress site hosting (although not all that advertise 'WordPress hosting' are set up specifically for it). I also know of one host that specializes in hosting WordPress sites that are built with the Genesis WordPress theme.

So, which should you go for?

Well, that will depend on how much money you have available for your hosting. If you have a good budget, I would recommend going with a true 'WordPress optimized' web host. Here are two of the better-known options:

1. WPEngine
2. WebSynthesis - This is hosting specifically designed for StudioPress themes (Genesis Framework), which are really popular Wordpress themes.

Links to both of these can be found on the book resource page here:

http://ezseonews.com/wpseo

If you visit those hosts, you'll notice that they are quite pricey, starting at $29/$47 per month for a single website. I have never used these personally, so cannot comment on their reliability. I do suggest you read the small print for whatever hosting package you decide to go with. The first host listed above has a price of $29 per month, but that only allows you 25,000 visitors a month in traffic. That is less than 850 visits a day, and for big, popular sites would be a problem.

If you are on a budget, then shared hosting may be a better option. I use shared hosting for a lot of my own sites, and the one I recommend is really good.

2.1. CDN (Content Delivery Network)

CDN stands for Content Delivery Network. The name gives you a very good idea what this does. It's a network of computers that deliver content. In this case, web pages.

Here is the definition of a CDN from Wikipedia:

> A content delivery network or content distribution network (**CDN**) is a globally distributed network of proxy servers deployed in multiple data centers. The goal of a **CDN** is to serve content to end-users with high availability and high performance.
>
> Content delivery network - Wikipedia
> https://en.wikipedia.org/wiki/Content_delivery_network

That's a little technical. Here is another definition from Webopedia:

> A **content delivery network (CDN)** is a system of distributed servers (network) that deliver webpages and other Web content to a user based on the geographic locations of the user, the origin of the webpage and a content delivery server.
>
> What is Content Delivery Network (CDN)? Webopedia Definition
> www.webopedia.com/TERM/C/**CDN**.html

Again, that's a little technical.

The bottom line is that if your website uses a CDN, then your web page will be served from a number of computers around the world. If someone in Australia tries to view your web page, then the CDN will serve up a copy of your page from Australia. If someone in Germany tries to view your web page, the CDN will serve a copy of your page from Germany. By matching visitor location to CDN server, web page load speeds are minimized.

You should definitely use a CDN if you have access to one. It had a dramatic effect on both load times and reliability of my websites when I started using one. You'll see the actual server response time graphs from one of my own sites in the next section.

A CDN does not have to cost you anything. Some web hosts include one with the hosting plan. The web host I use and recommend does.

2.2. Shared Hosting & Dedicated Servers

Most hosts offer a wide range of packages, from simple shared hosting to dedicated servers (where you basically are given a computer and told to get on with it).

Dedicated servers, and unmanaged VPS hosting, both require a certain level of technical know-how, so I don't recommend you consider those unless you are technically capable.

For most people, shared hosting will be the best option because of the lower costs, especially for new sites. However, shared hosting is generally the most unreliable in terms of uptime and server response times (how long the server takes to respond to a request to show your web page).

I recommend you test any host you are considering working with. If you know of a website that is hosted with a particular company, I suggest you sign up for a website monitoring service and keep an eye on the website uptime and server response times (essentially how quick and reliable the web host is). Pingdom.com has a free 14-day trial, so you can use that to test a host. Monitis is another popular premium service that I personally use, but it no longer offers a free trial account.

Monitoring a website on a particular web host will give you a good idea of how reliable that hosting company actually is. You can find links to these services here:

http://ezseonews.com/wpseo

Two of the most popular shared hosting companies are Hostgator and Bluehost. I have tried both in the past and had several accounts at Hostgator. I moved away from Hostgator a few years back after they 'upgraded' the server I was on. The uptime and response times plummeted as a result. Here is a screenshot from Monitis showing the details for one of my Hostgator hosted websites:

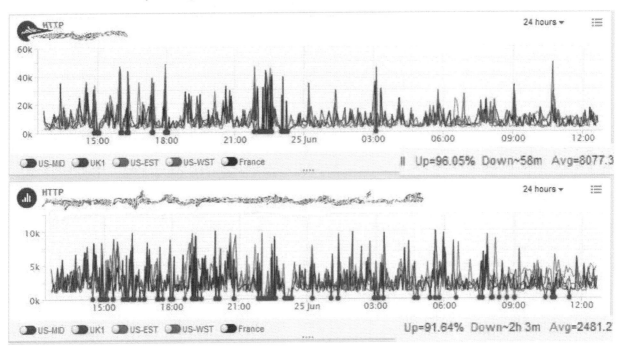

Look at all those peaks (peaks show when the server took longer to respond), and the small circular dots on the baseline (where the server did not respond).

The top graph is the homepage of the site. Over a 24-hour period, the homepage was down for 58 minutes, and the server response time was over eight seconds! That means it took eight seconds on average (although there are a lot of peaks over 40 seconds), to connect to my server, and that's even before the web page started to download.

The lower graph is an internal page on the same site. This page gets less traffic so should have better response times - which it does - at around 2.5 seconds. However, that page was down for over two hours in the previous 24 hours.

I moved this site from Hostgator to Bluehost, but I found Bluehost to be just as unreliable. I guess Hostgator and Bluehost (being two of the most popular shared hosting companies) have suffered because of their own success.

I eventually found a host that I am happy with called StableHost. I have been with Stablehost ever since.

If you are interested, read my comparative review. In it, I show the site load times as I move a real site from Hostgator over to Stablehost:

http://ezseonews.com/stablehostreview

StableHost offers free CDN with their hosting (which basically means your site is served from a network of servers around the globe). My test site is hosted on their Enterprise hosting package, costing $29.95 per month at the time or writing, but I have also done tests on their basic shared hosting and been very happy with the results (see that link above).

The site had CDN enabled (free with Stablehost hosting packages and only takes two minutes to set up).

Here is a screenshot showing response times before and after the move from Hostgator to Stablehost:

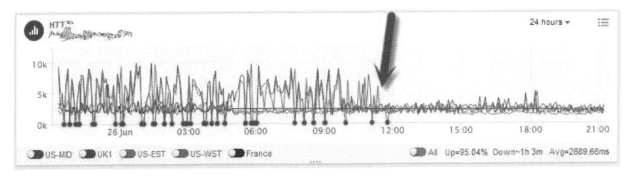

Before the arrow is Hostgator and after the arrow is Stablehost!

After the move, here is the data from Monitis over a 24-hour period.

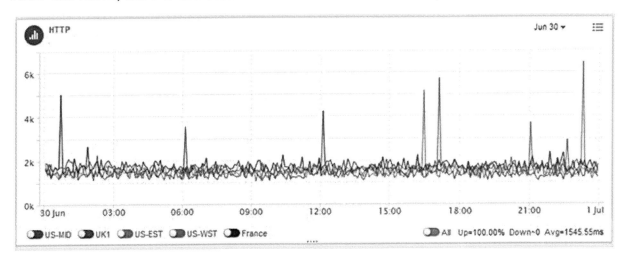

That's 100% uptime and a response time of around 1.5 seconds on average.

Here is an inner page:

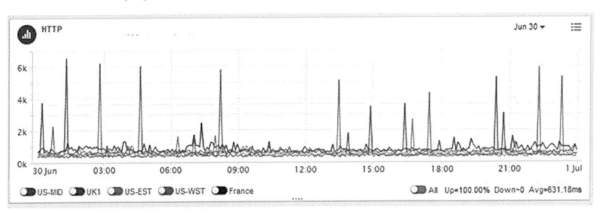

Another 100% uptime and response time was 0.65 seconds.

You'll notice that there were far fewer peaks in response times on StableHost. When there were peaks, it was a maximum of around 6 seconds, compared to the 40+ second peaks on Hostgator.

What all of this shows you, I hope, is that not all hosts are equal. If you want reliable hosting, go for the best that you can afford (and remember price does not necessarily correlate with quality). My order of choice would be:

1. WPEngine OR WebSynthesis (but I would still test them).

2. Enterprise level hosting on StableHost, using CDN.

3. Shared hosting, using CDN, but choose a good host like Stablehost.

NOTE: If you do decide to try Stablehost, make sure you read my comparative review. It includes a 40% discount coupon for new customers on Stablehost.

3. Themes & Theme Settings

There are lots of great themes out there, many of them are free. I don't generally recommend free themes, and here's why:

- They may not get updated.

- Some might include malicious code.

- A number of them contain footer links back to the creator's website (or any website they choose), which is really bad for SEO.

- They could be poorly written, and therefore slow to load.

Themes are very much a personal choice and depend on the type of site you are building. It is, therefore, difficult for me to recommend a theme to you. However, to get you started, check out these two that I often use myself:

1. Genesis Framework and associated child themes.

2. Customizr Pro.

Links to both can be found at http://ezseonews.com/wpseo

Genesis is a 'framework'. Essentially a framework powers your WordPress site, and you change the appearance of your site by installing child themes, or skins that work with the framework.

When you come to choose a theme, there is a checklist to take into consideration:

The theme MUST:

1. load quickly.

2. allows you to control how posts appear on all of the six 'potential duplication areas' of your site that we looked at earlier. You should have the options of a full post, excerpt, or just the title.

3. have at least one sidebar.

4. allow one (or two) menus at the top of the website.

5. not include any mandatory links or attributions in the footer.

Points 2-5 can be answered by the theme's support desk. What about the first point, though? How can you tell the load speed of a website, and check for potential problems with a template? You'll be pleased to know that this can be done quickly and simply.

For this, we can use a free service at GTMetrix.com

GTMetrix allows you to analyze the page load times of any web page you want.

Find a site that uses the theme you are interested in using, and enter the URL of that site into GTMetrix. This tool then breaks down the page load speed into elements and tells you exactly how long each element takes to load.

First the summary:

The summary gives you an A, B, C, D or E rating for page speed. You also get to see the page load time in seconds, the total page size, and the number of requests that were needed to download the page.

You should be trying to get an A or B for PageSpeed Score. Obviously the lower the page load time, the better. I typically try for under 2 seconds if at all possible. The page in the screenshot above takes 4.4 seconds, which is a little slow.

Under the main summary are 5 tabs: PageSpeed, YSlow, Waterfall, Video and History.

The Page Speed and YSlow tabs offer advice on how to speed up the website. Click on any entry in these tables for an expanded view that shows you specifically what you need to do to fix an issue.

The waterfall tab offers an interesting view of the page load speed. It tells you exactly how long each element on the page took to load. This is where you can get information on any 'theme-specific' problems.

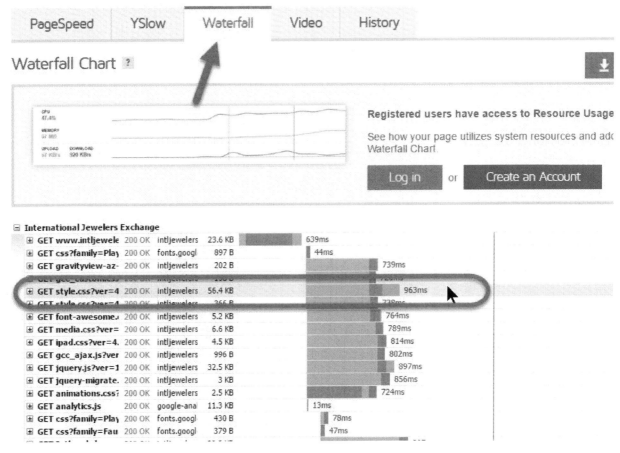

On the right-hand side, you can see the times taken to load each element. The timings are in milliseconds (1000ms equals one second).

On the left-hand side, you get a list of the page elements. If you move your mouse over an element, it will expand to show you the full URL of that component. For example, the element below took nearly a second to load:

In this case, it tells me that the element is the CSS file (style sheet) for the Avada theme.

By looking for slow loading elements on the page, and checking whether they are related to the theme you want to use, you can make judgments on the how well that theme is optimized.

TIP: You will find that a lot of the slower loading elements on a page are images. Some images are related to the theme, whereas others are not. Don't worry about slow loading images that are not part of the theme.

Also, look for any element that has a large file size as these take longer to download. There is a column that shows you the size of each element. Be careful, though, as some of these are in bytes (B) whereas others are in KB (Kilobytes, or 1000 bytes):

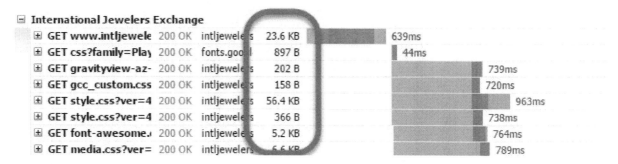

One final thing to be mindful of is that it's unlikely the demo sites set up by theme vendors use caching plugins, or a content delivery network (CDN). That means the speeds you see with tools like this will probably be faster once it is set up on your server and properly optimized. With this in mind, don't concentrate too much on the page load times reported, and instead, look for large files that the theme uses, as these may cause speed problems on *any* server.

Hopefully, you have seen that choosing a theme is not just as simple as finding one that looks good and using it. You need to make sure it will load fast too, and not contribute to longer loading times, especially if you go with cheaper, shared hosting.

Once you have chosen a theme and installed it, I recommend you **uninstall** all other themes that may be in your WordPress Dashboard. The reason for this is that old themes can often be routes taken by hackers to gain access to your site. We really don't want to give them that chance!

Summary: Delete all themes (and plugins), that you are not using.

4. Google Tools

Google offer some great tools and advice to the webmaster, for free. I use them, and I recommend you do too. The two recommended tools are:

☐ Google Search Console (previously called Google Webmaster Tools).

☐ Google Analytics.

I also recommend you read and learn Google's Webmaster Guidelines.

Links to all of these can be found on the resource page for this book, here:

http://ezseonews.com/wpseo

4.1 Google Search Console

Why should you use Google Search Console (GSC)?

Here are some good reasons:

- Get notified by Google if there is a problem with your site. Google will send you messages if for example, your backlink profile looks spammy, or if your site is using an old version of WordPress, etc. It will also notify you if it detects malware on your website.

- Discover any HTML problems with your site. You can then follow the suggestions that GSC gives you to resolve the issue(s).

- Submit and check your sitemap (which can speed up indexing of your website).

- Select a geographic target audience. For example, if your website targets UK customers, but your site uses a .com extension, you can use GSC to tell Google that you want your site to be given more consideration in the UK.

- Check how well your site is being indexed by Google.

- Identify crawl errors. Google will tell you the URLs that it had trouble crawling, and the page which linked to that URL, thus allowing you to quickly identify and fix broken links on your site.

- Request Google removes specific URLs from their search results.

- Get a complete list of all links that point to your website (at least the ones that Google knows about). This can be very useful, especially in identifying links from spammy sites, which you can then disavow with the Google Disavow tool.

- Identify keywords that people are using to find your site. Google shows you the number of impressions in the search engines, how many clicks you got, the click-through rate (CTR), and average position in the SERPs (Search Engine Results Pages). The CTR can be very useful for finding pages that may need their title/description tweaked so as to try and improve the CTR.

GSC offers a useful set of tools for all webmasters. I highly recommend you sign up and add your website(s) to your account, so you can track them all.

4.2 Google Analytics

Google Analytics is a free visitor tracking tool, which is far more powerful than many commercial tools that are available.

Reasons to use Google Analytics (GA) include:

- See details of your visitors, like the search term they used to find your site, how long they spent on your site, which browser they use, what country they come from, and so on.

- Get real-time statistics, showing how many people are on your site right now, and which pages they are viewing, etc.

- Connect your Google Analytics account to your GSC account, and Google AdSense account, for even more tracking features.

- Split-test different versions of, for example, a sales page.

- Set up custom alerts, to notify you about the things that are important to your business.

- Monitor mobile traffic.

- Lots of other features...

Once you have signed up for Google Analytics and registered your site with them, you'll be given some tracking code to insert into your web pages. Some themes will have an easy way to add in your Google Analytics code, while others won't.

If you cannot find an easy way to add the tracking code, I would recommend you look for a Wordpress plugin called "Header and Footer". This plugin will let you insert the code into the header or footer of every page on your site. I like this particular plugin because it has a lot of other features I regularly find useful (like inserting code before, after, or within a post/page's content).

4.3 Google's Webmaster Guidelines

Google's Webmaster Guidelines is a collection of articles detailing exactly what Google likes, and dislikes. If you own a website, you should be reading these guidelines and taking notes.

You can find a link to the guidelines here:

http://ezseonews.com/wpseo

The Webmaster Guidelines are divided into several sections:

☐ General Guidelines - advice on how you can make sure Google finds and understands your pages.

☐ Quality Guidelines – SEO advice including what not to do. A lot of the Wordpress SEO advice I'll give you in this book relates directly to these guidelines. They are VERY important.

5. Screen Options

The WordPress Dashboard has some settings hidden away in the top right-hand corner of the screen. You should see the **Screen Options** tab:

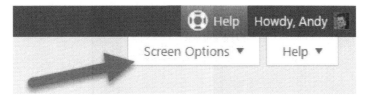

The screen options are not available everywhere inside the Dashboard, so if you don't see the **Screen options** tab, click on the Dashboard link in the side menu. It will then appear.

The screen options control what you see on the screen when you are moving around the dashboard. They offer a series of "switches" to turn on/off elements of the Dashboard.

These screen options change depending on where you are in the dashboard, so they are always specific to the task at hand. For example, if you are editing a post, the screen options will be related to adding posts:

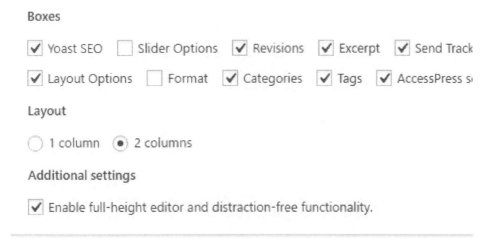

If there is something you do not use, uncheck it and it disappears from your dashboard, helping to reduce any unnecessary clutter. Plugins can add items to the screen options, so if you don't see the same items as in my screenshot, that is fine.

As another example, here are the screen options I get when I am moderating comments:

Columns

☑ Author ☑ In Response To ☑ Submitted On

Pagination

Number of items per page: 20

[Apply]

If you are ever looking for something mentioned in this book, or any other, but don't see it in your dashboard, then check the screen options. There's a good chance you have that particular box unchecked.

6. WordPress Settings Menu

During the initial setup of a WordPress site, it's a good idea to go through the Settings menu first to make sure everything is set up properly. You will find this settings menu in the left sidebar of your Dashboard. Mouse-over the word 'Settings' and a popup menu will appear displaying the options. Click on the word 'Settings' and that menu integrates into the sidebar, below the main Settings heading.

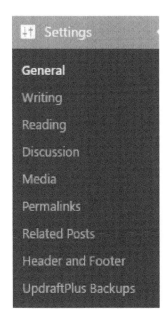

As with the screen options, plugins can add items to this **Settings** menu. You can see three items at the bottom of my settings that have been added by plugins (related posts, header, and footer & updraftplus backups).

Once we install a few plugins, later on, your settings menu will start to fill out too.

Let's go through the settings that are relevant to SEO.

6.1. General Settings

Site Title & Tagline

The top two items in the General settings are Site Title and Tagline. The Site Title and Tagline entered here will be displayed at the top of every page on your site. You can replace this with a logo image if you want, but how to do that will depend on the theme you are using. Each theme will have slightly different instructions for adding a logo and logo dimensions will also be theme specific.

Don't be tempted to stuff keywords into the site name or tagline fields. Your site name will most probably be based on your domain name, and the tagline should be a short sentence specifying your site's goal, philosophy or slogan.

There is a good article on creating a tagline on the Copyblogger website called "How to Create a Rock-Solid Tagline That Truly Works". Read it here:

http://www.copyblogger.com/create-a-tagline/

If you need help with yours, I suggest you read that.

E-mail Address

The only other setting we need to concern ourselves with on this page is the email address. This will be used by WordPress, plugins, and a free external service

(Gravatar.com). We'll be looking at these later, so your email address needs to be correct.

6.2. Writing Settings

In terms of SEO, the only setting we need to change here is the **Update Services**. These are a list of web services that get notified whenever new content gets published on your site. Having a good 'ping list' will help your content get indexed more quickly.

Search Google for "WordPress ping list" and you'll find a list of sites to include. Simply copy and paste the list into the Update Services box, and then save your settings.

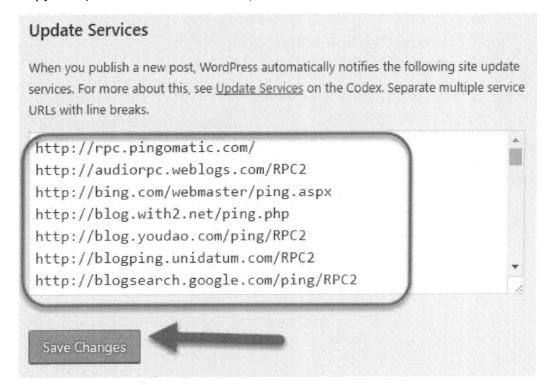

6.3. Reading Settings

Latest posts vs. static page

If you have not published any Wordpress Pages (pages, not posts) on your site, then you will see this:

Reading Settings

Blog pages show at most	`10`	posts
Syndication feeds show the most recent	`10`	items
For each article in a feed, show	⦿ Full text ◯ Summary	
Search Engine Visibility	☐ Discourage search engines from indexing this site *It is up to search engines to honor this request.*	

Save Changes

If you have published at least one page, then you will see this at the top of the settings:

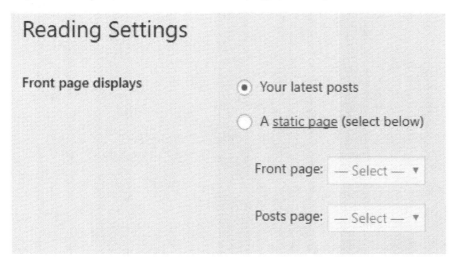

The **"Front page displays"** settings allow you to define what is shown on your homepage. If you have published a page, you can use that page as your homepage. Hence the reason these options are only available if you have a page published.

You actually have two options to use for the homepage on your site. You can select:

1. Your latest posts

2. A static page

If you select **a static page** as your homepage, then you will be required to select the Wordpress page in the drop down box.

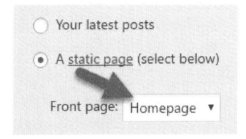

To make things easier for myself, I always name the page I am going to use as my homepage, "Homepage".

Next up on the Reading Settings is deciding how many posts to display on the archive pages (like category page, author page, etc.), and decide what information is shown in RSS feeds (something WordPress generates for your site).

Blog pages show at most	10	posts
Syndication feeds show the most recent	10	items
For each article in a feed, show	◯ Full text	
	◉ Summary	
Search Engine Visibility	☐ Discourage search engines from indexing this site	
	It is up to search engines to honor this request.	

Save Changes

The default setting is 10, which means WordPress will show 10 posts on the homepage (if the homepage uses "latest posts", 10 on the category pages, and 10 on the author page, etc. If there are more than 10 posts to show, then the remainder will be added, in batches of 10, to additional pages, and you'll get a next/previous type navigation to move between them.

I would recommend you leave the '**Blog pages show at most**' set to 10.

Beneath that is the '**Syndication feeds show the most recent**' option.

WordPress creates RSS feeds for your site. Your site will have a main feed, plus there will be feeds for category pages, tag pages, and so on. This setting tells WordPress how many items to include in the feed. With Google's Penguin algorithm looking at the over-optimization of inbound links, I'd limit the RSS feed to a maximum of 10. In the past, webmasters have included 100 items (or more), and that would mean any site that is displaying your RSS feed will contain 100 links back to it. Before Google Penguin, that was OK, but not now. Leave this number set at 10.

You now have to decide what the feed contains, i.e., all the content of your posts, or just a summary of them. Select **Summary.** Otherwise, you are making if far too easy for scraper software tools to copy (steal), your content. These software tools monitor RSS feeds and strip the content out. Your content is then likely to be posted on one or more spammy sites around the internet, and that's not good.

Another reason to limit this to 10 is simply that RSS feeds are great for getting content indexed quickly. You only really need the last 10 items published on your site in the feed. Once these are indexed in the search engines, there is no need for them to still be in the feed. As more content is added to your site, they will scroll off the bottom of the feed and be replaced by newer content, ready for indexing.

The final option on this page is '**Search Engine Visibility**'. When some people develop a website, they want it to be finished before the search engines come to spider the site. This option allows you to do just that. By checking the box, your website will basically tell the search engines to ignore it until you decide the time is right, and uncheck this option.

I recommend you leave this box unchecked from the start, that's unless you have good reason to not want the content indexed as you create it. As I add content to a website, I *want* Google to find and index it as soon as possible. If it sees new content being added regularly, it'll know the site is active and needs to be spidered more regularly to keep their index up to date. By leaving this option unchecked, you are encouraging the search engine spiders to crawl your site, and that's a good thing.

6.4 Discussion Settings

The Discussion Settings refer to the commenting system built into WordPress.

Google likes to see visitor interaction on a website, so this is an important part of your WordPress SEO. You'll want to keep the comments enabled.

At the top of these settings, you will see:

Discussion Settings

Default article settings

- ✔ Attempt to notify any blogs linked to from the article
- ✔ Allow link notifications from other blogs (pingbacks and trackbacks) on new articles
- ✔ Allow people to post comments on new articles

(These settings may be overridden for individual articles.)

These boxes should all be left checked.

The first option means WordPress will try to send a notification to any blog you link to in your posts. This lets a site owner know you have linked to them, and can sometimes result in a link back.

The second option is the first one in reverse. If someone links to your site, then WordPress will notify you so that you can see who's linking to you. This has been abused by spammers and you will get a lot of false positives here, but it is worth checking out these notifications to see if someone is talking about you.

The final option simply tells WordPress to allow visitors to comment on your posts. This is what we want – visitor participation.

The '**Other comment settings**' section has a few more options:

Other comment settings

☑ Comment author must fill out name and email

☐ Users must be registered and logged in to comment

☐ Automatically close comments on articles older than [14] days

☑ Enable threaded (nested) comments [5 ▾] levels deep

☐ Break comments into pages with [50] top level comments per page and the

[last ▾]
page displayed by default

Comments should be displayed with the
[older ▾]
comments at the top of each page

Check the first box so that anyone leaving a comment must enter a name and an email address.

The second box should be unchecked unless you are creating some kind of membership site where people need to register in order to participate.

Leave the third box unchecked too, unless there is a reason why you want to close comments on older posts. I personally like to keep comments open indefinitely, and if there is a post where I want to close them, I can do that on the 'Edit Post' screen, just for that one post.

The fourth checkbox will enable nested comments. This is something that not only makes the comments look better but more intuitive for your visitors. This is because replies to a specific comment will be nested under the original, and this, in turn, makes following the conversation much easier.

The next option allows you to spread comments across pages once you get over a certain number of remarks on the main post page. This is a good idea if your site gets a lot of comments, because the more you have, the longer the page will take to load. If you anticipate a lot of comments, enable this option. You can also specify here whether you want comments to be shown with the oldest or newest first. I personally think it makes more sense to have older comments at the top. That way, the comments are chronological, but this is a personal preference.

Next on this page is the 'E-mail me whenever' settings. Do you want to be notified when someone comments on a post? If so, make sure that option is checked. I recommend you check this so that you get instant notifications of any new comments posted on your site. This means you get to reply quickly. Fast responses to comments are important, and it makes the visitor feel that you care. Practicing good interaction means there's a much better chance the commenter will come back and visit your site again.

The second email option is to notify you when a comment is held for moderation. You can uncheck this, because in a moment we will tell WordPress to hold ALL comments for moderation, and we are already getting notified every time someone posts a comment anyway.

In the '**Before a comment appears**' section, check the first box, and uncheck the second.

Before a comment appears

☑ Comment must be manually approved

☐ Comment author must have a previously approved comment

This will force ALL comments to appear in a moderation queue, and will only go live on your site once you approve them.

This means the next couple of settings in the '**Comment Moderation**' section are irrelevant since ALL comments are now held for moderation. We can, therefore, ignore that section.

NOTE: Moderating comments might sound like a lot of work, but it is essential. If you have your site set up to auto-approve comments, your pages will end up full of spam remarks and possible security loopholes added by hackers trying to gain access. Needless to say, that would take a lot more time cleaning up than moderating comments.

The '**Comment Blacklist**' is a good way to fight spam. You can include email addresses, IP addresses, and certain words in the box. If a comment matches any of those lines, it is automatically marked as spam. If I end up getting a lot of spam comments from a particular IP address, I usually add that to this list as well.

You can search Google for a "WordPress comment blacklist" which will get you started. Just add one item per line, and save your changes when done.

The final section on the Discussion Settings relates to the use of "Avatars".

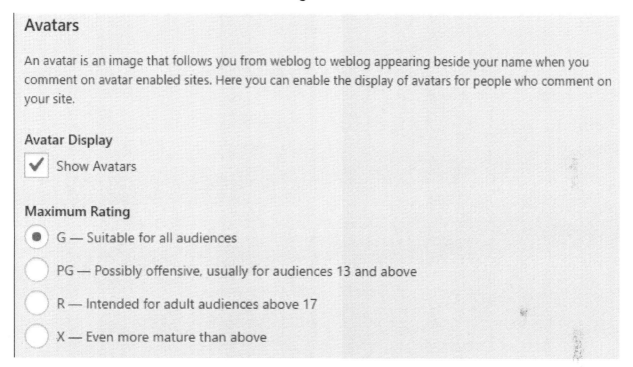

An Avatar is a small image of the author. If the author of a comment has a Gravatar (http://gravatar.com/) assigned to the email address, and they use that same email to leave a comment, then that Gravatar is shown as their avatar.

I recommend you check '**Show Avatars**'. I think this helps the comment section become more active since visitors to your site can see little photos of real people leaving remarks. Site visitors like to know who they are dealing with, a face behind the name as it were, so these images help instill confidence and help gain site credibility.

I would also recommend you check the 'G' rating so the avatars on your site should be suitable viewing for all ages.

In the **Default** Avatar section, select '**Blank**'. Avatars take time to load, thus increasing the page load time. With blank selected, if a person does not have a Gravatar set up, no image is loaded for that person. If you leave it at the default "Mystery Person", that mystery person image will be loaded whenever someone leaves a comment and does not have a Gravatar set up.

6.5. Media Settings

While the settings here allow us to determine the default sizes of images in posts, I recommend you do that manually on a post by post basis at the time you create them. Therefore, there are no specific settings in the Media Settings section that we need to change for SEO purposes.

6.6 Permalinks Settings

The Permalink settings are important because whatever you enter here will influence the way the URLs are displayed for the pages on your website.

The "Plain" WordPress setting will produce URLs like this:

mydomain.com/?p=123

The '**?p=123**' parameter in this URL is simply a call for the page with Page ID = 123. This is not very useful for visitors, it looks ugly, and it's certainly not helpful to search engines.

The default option for permalinks is "Day and Name", but this creates URLs like this:

mydomain.com/2016/12/23/hello-world/

Do you really want the date of the post in the URL? Some news sites or sites where the date is important may do, but for most sites, this just alerts your visitors to the fact that a post is getting a little old.

A lot of people will use the 'post name' option, which uses the post title in the URL.

mydomain.com/hello-world/

Actually, it uses the post 'slug' which is equivalent to the post "filename" on HTML websites. Usually, the slug is the post title unless you change it. For example, if you had a post called 'Liverpool win in Istanbul', then by default the URL for that post would look like this:

mydomain.com/liverpool-win-in-istanbul

Note that capitals are stripped out and spaces are replaced by dashes. Some other characters will also be removed, like apostrophes.

I actually recommend you use a permalink structure that contains the category of the post. To do this, choose '**Custom Structure**' and enter the following as your permalink structure:

/%category%/%postname%/

Here it is in my settings:

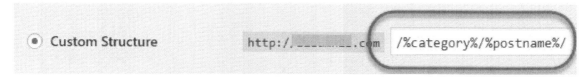

Now the URL of any page will include the category and filename of the post. A typical URL for a post might look like this:

mydomain.com/dog-breeds/alsatians

In this instance, the post filename is 'Alsatians', and the post is in the 'dog breeds' category.

IMPORTANT:

With Google's Panda and Penguin looking for what Google calls 'webspam', we need to be very careful about choosing the correct category names for our site, especially if we are including the category in the URL.

For example, if your site is called mydietreviews.com, and you had a category called 'diets', then the URL might look like this:

my**diet**reviews.com/**diets**/hollywood-**diet**/

This URL has the word 'diet' in it three times. That could well be seen as keyword stuffing and should be avoided. If you think that this type of situation will arise on your site with the categories you have chosen, then play it safe and use the "post name" permalink structure instead.

At the bottom of the permalink settings, there are some optional choices:

Optional

If you like, you may enter custom structures for your category and tag URLs here. For example, using `topi` base would make your category links like `http://          i.com/topics/uncategorized/`. If you leav will be used.

Category base

Tag base

To understand what these options do, I need to tell you how WordPress assigns the URL for category pages and tag pages.

Every category page will have the word 'category' in the URL and every tag page will have the word 'tag' in the URL. Therefore, using the examples above, the category page URL would look like this:

mydietreviews.com/**category**/diets/

This category page will then show all the posts in the diets category.

Similarly, a tag page URL would look something like this:

mydietreviews.com/**tag**/fat-loss/

Any posts on your site that were tagged with the term 'fat loss' would be listed on this page.

With that knowledge, let's go back to the "category base" and "tag base" settings.

If you leave these empty, then category and tag page URLs will be created as described above, with the word "category" or "tag" inserted into the URL.

If you prefer to use a different word than "category" or "tag" for these URLs, you can enter it in the "category base" and "tag base" settings.

For example, if you set the category base to 'abracadabra', then the category URL would become:

mydietreviews.com/**abracadabra**/diets/

Before Panda and Penguin, category and tag bases were used to keyword stuff the URLs. Today, leave them blank as they will only get your site into trouble.

It is also possible to remove the word "category" altogether from category page URLs using a plugin that we'll look at later. This is not an option for tag page URLs.

7. Plugins

Before we look at the plugins, I need to mention that many are updated frequently and their appearance can change a little as a consequence. That means the screenshots in this book may not be identical to what you are seeing in your Dashboard. Most changes are minor, though, so you should still be able to set everything up properly, even if your plugin is a different version to the one that I am showing in this book.

What I am going to do in this section is get you to install certain plugins. We won't go through the configuration of each one just yet; we'll do that later in the book when we need to achieve certain SEO goals.

There are a few essential plugins to get your WordPress site ready for the search engines. I'll cover these first, and I recommend you install ALL three of them. I'll then list a few other plugins that you may find useful, and explain what they do. You can hold off installing these until you know whether you will need them or not.

To install the plugins, login to the Dashboard, and from the left side column, go to Plugins -> Add New. You will see a search box & button. Enter the plugin names in the search box as I state them below, and then install and activate each one.

7.1. Essential Plugins

1. Yoast SEO

This is a comprehensive SEO plugin that will create a self-updating sitemap and allow us fine control over the SEO of the site.

Search for "Yoast SEO".

This is the one you are looking for, by Team Joost:

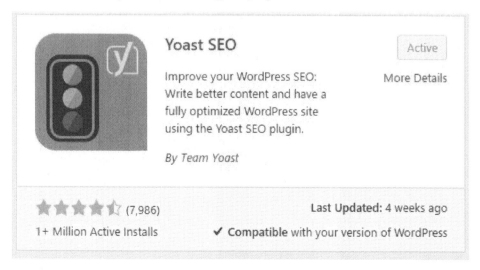

Click the Install now link, and once installed, activate the plugin.

2. W3 Total Cache

This plugin is essential because it speeds up your website. Page load speed, as mentioned previously, is an important part of SEO. Google like fast loading pages, and once we have this plugin configured, your site should load several times faster than before.

Search for "W3 Total Cache".

This is the one you are looking for, by Frederick Townes:

Install and activate the plugin.

3. Dynamic Widgets

The final essential plugin is called Dynamic Widgets, and this allows us to create dynamic, context-sensitive sidebars (and other elements), on our website.

Search for "dynamic widgets", and look for this one by Qurl:

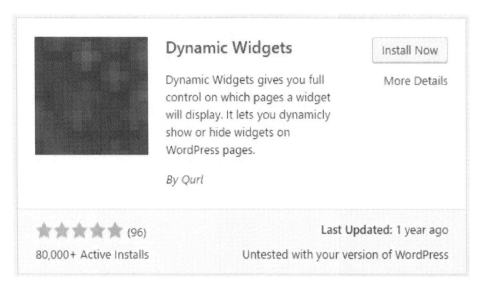

Install and activate the plugin.

That's it. Those are the three essential plugins we need to set up for SEO purposes.

7.2 Non-essential Plugins

I won't be going into details on installing and configuring these non-essential plugins. I will just tell you what they do, and if you want to add them to your site, you can use the help documents that come with them should you need assistance setting them up.

Remember this, though. The more plugins you install on your site, the slower it will potentially load. Therefore, keep plugins to a minimum, and only use ones that you actually need.

1. YARPP

YARPP stands for 'Yet Another Related Posts Plugin'. It basically creates a list of related posts, dynamically, for each post on your site. These posts can be automatically inserted after a post's content, or you can insert related posts as a widget, meaning you can place them into any widgetized area of your template, for example, a sidebar.

Search for "yarpp"

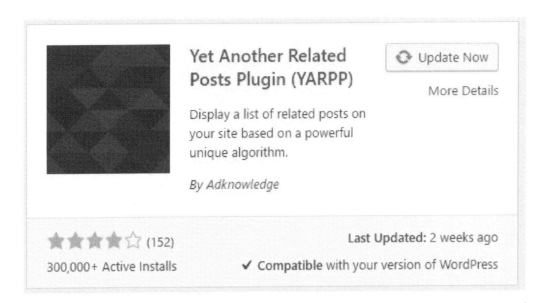

Yet Another Related Posts Plugin (YARPP)

Display a list of related posts on your site based on a powerful unique algorithm.

By Adknowledge

Update Now

More Details

★★★★☆ (152)

300,000+ Active Installs

Last Updated: 2 weeks ago

✔ Compatible with your version of WordPress

2. Contact form 7

This plugin makes it easy to set up a contact form on your site. A contact form is an essential part of any website. Whether or not you expect your visitors to contact you, the search engines expect good sites to have this option.

Search for "contact form 7"

Contact Form 7

Just another contact form plugin. Simple but flexible.

By Takayuki Miyoshi

Active

More Details

★★★★☆ (1,076)

1+ Million Active Installs

Last Updated: 1 month ago

✔ Compatible with your version of WordPress

3. UpdraftPlus

Updraft Plus has a free and premium version. For most people, the free version is all you'll need. This plugin will automatically backup your site on a schedule you choose. It will also help you restore your site from backup if you ever need to. UpdraftPlus can backup to S3, Dropbox, Google Drive, email, and other places.

Search for " updraftplus"

4. Broken Link Checker

If your site has a lot out outbound links to other websites (by the way, linking to authority sites within your niche is a good idea), then this plugin can check your outbound links and tell you if any are broken. Google don't like broken links on a site and may punish you if you have a lot of them. Therefore, this plugin can help ensure this does not become a problem.

Search for "broken link checker"

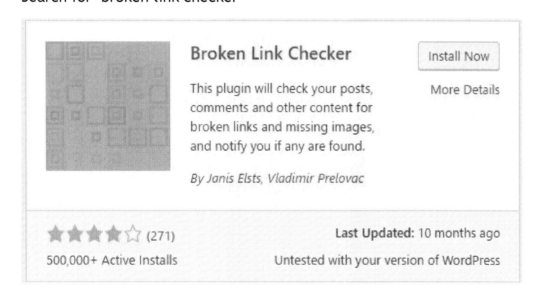

5. Social Media Flying Icons

Social Media Flying Icons adds stylish, floating social media sharing buttons to your site. There are a lot of social media sharing button plugins around, so try out a few. I have included this one in the book because it is regularly updated, popular and has great reviews. The plugin has a perfectly usable free version and a premium version for those that want the extra features.

Search for "floating social media"

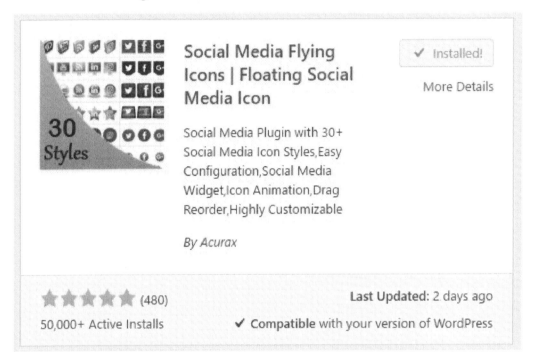

6. Stop Spammers Spam Prevention

Wordpress comes pre-installed with Akismet, a great anti-comment spam plugin. However, it is not free for commercial use. If you want a free plugin, try Stop Spammers Spam Prevention. Search for "stop spammers" and look for this one:

Stop Spammers Spam Prevention

Install Now

More Details

Aggressive anti-spam plugin that eliminates comment spam, trackback spam, contact form spam and registration spam. Protects against malicious attacks.

By Keith P. Graham

★★★★☆ (147)

30,000+ Active Installs

Last Updated: 9 months ago

Untested with your version of WordPress

7. Pretty Link Lite

Pretty Link Lite is a free plugin (there is a commercial version too, but the free version is all most people need). What this plugin does, is allow you to set up redirects on your site. Therefore, if you want to use an affiliate link on your page(s), you could set up a link like mydomain.com/affproduct, and this would redirect to the affiliate site. Why bother? If you don't know why you would want to do this, then you most probably don't need this plugin. One other nice feature is that it tracks clicks on all of the pretty links you set up, which can be very useful.

Search for "pretty link lite"

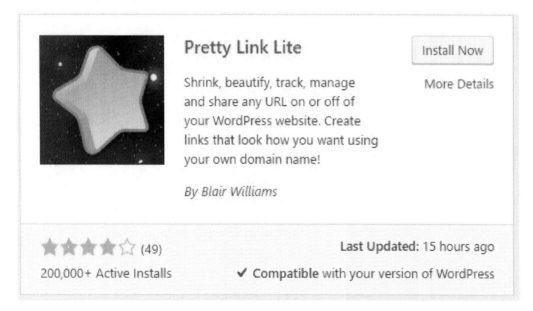

Pretty Link Lite

Install Now

More Details

Shrink, beautify, track, manage and share any URL on or off of your WordPress website. Create links that look how you want using your own domain name!

By Blair Williams

★★★★☆ (49)

200,000+ Active Installs

Last Updated: 15 hours ago

✔ **Compatible** with your version of WordPress

8. All in One Security & Firewall

This is a comprehensive, free, security plugin that will protect your site against hackers. Search for "all in one security" and look for this plugin:

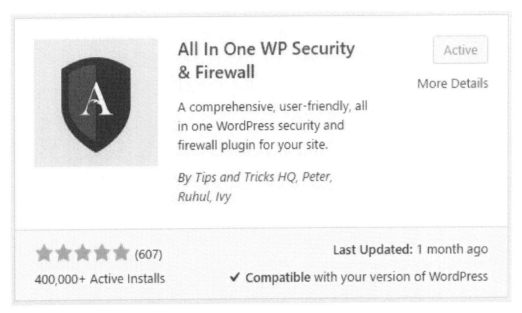

9. CI Backlinks

This plugin allows you automate the internal linking of content across your site. It is a plugin I use on all of my websites because internal linking done manually is an almost impossible task. For example, when you add a new post to your website, you'd need to go and find all other posts that mention that topic so an internal link can be created. With this plugin, you set up the rules and internal links are updated automatically as you add new content.

More details from http://ezseonews.com/wpseo

OK, that brings an end to my list of essential, and not so essential, plugins. Make sure you get the essentials installed before moving on. We'll be starting to configure them very soon.

8. Keeping WordPress Up to Date - WordPress & Plugins

It is important that you always keep WordPress and plugins up to date. Hackers typically look for exploits in WordPress, so updates fix any known problems, thus keeping your website protected.

Wordpress will actually auto-update minor versions of Wordpress for you, making sure your site is always protected. Occasionally, when major versions are released, you will need to go in and manually update your installation.

If a WordPress or plugin update is available, you'll see a red circle with a number inside, next to the Updates menu on the Dashboard:

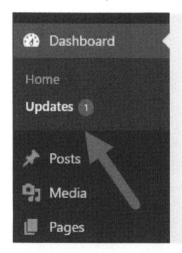

Click on '**Updates**' to be taken to the updates screen. This can have up to three sections. At the very top, if a WordPress update is available, you'll see an option to install it.

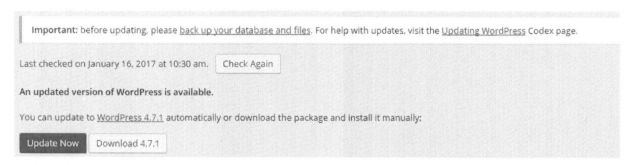

Under that, if plugins are available for update, you'll see them here. Simply check the plugins you want to update, and then click the '**Update Plugins**' button.

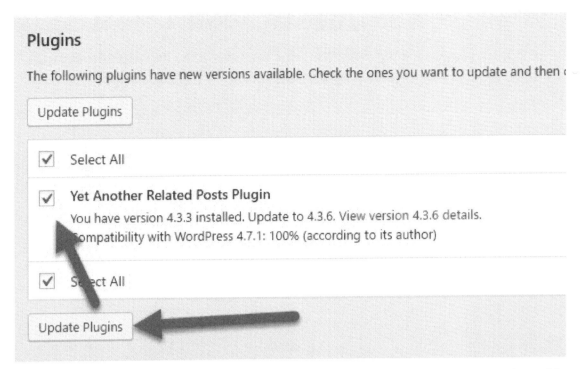

At the bottom of the page, if a theme has an update, you should see it listed here too (though that will depend on the theme and where you got it from). Again, check the theme(s) you want to update, and click the 'Update Themes' button.

9. Duplication on Category, Tag & Other Archive Pages

As mentioned at the beginning of this book, these pages are the root of many SEO problems. Let me show you an example of this.

I've created a dummy post for a fictitious gift website. The post is called 'Gift ideas for children', and it's in a category called 'children'.

After posting the article, here is my homepage:

Home   Sample Page

Gift ideas for children

Posted on July 3, 2013

These are gift ideas for children. These are gift ideas for children. These are gift ideas for children. These are gift ideas for children. These are gift ideas for children. These are gift ideas for children. These are gift ideas for children. These are gift ideas for children. These are gift ideas for children.

These are gift ideas for children. These are gift ideas for children. These are gift ideas for children. These are gift ideas for children. These are gift ideas for children. These are gift ideas for children.

These are gift ideas for children. These are gift ideas for children. These are gift ideas for children. These are gift ideas for children. These are gift ideas for children. These are gift ideas for children. These are gift ideas for children. These are gift ideas for children. These are gift ideas for children. These are gift ideas for children. These are gift ideas for children.

These are gift ideas for children. These are gift ideas for children. These are gift ideas for children. These are gift ideas for children. These are gift ideas for children.

Posted in Children | Leave a reply   Edit

The title of the post is actually a hyperlink that will open a page which contains an exact copy of the article. That means we now have two identical copies of the same post, but that's only the tip of the iceberg.

Look at the screenshot above under the title where it says 'Posted on July 3, 2013'. That date is a hyperlink to the date archive. Clicking on it takes me to a page that shows all posts that were published on that date. Here it is:

Home   Sample Page

Posted on July 3, 2013

Edit

Gift ideas for children

These are gift ideas for children. These are gift ideas for children. These are gift ideas for children. These are gift ideas for children. These are gift ideas for children. These are gift ideas for children. These are gift ideas for children. These are gift ideas for children. These are gift ideas for children.

These are gift ideas for children. These are gift ideas for children. These are gift ideas for children. These are gift ideas for children. These are gift ideas for children. These are gift ideas for children.

These are gift ideas for children. These are gift ideas for children. These are gift ideas for children. These are gift ideas for children. These are gift ideas for children. These are gift ideas for children. These are gift ideas for children. These are gift ideas for children. These are gift ideas for children. These are gift ideas for children. These are gift ideas for children.

The same full post again.

Go back to the homepage screenshot. See at the bottom of the post where it says 'Posted in children'. 'Children' is the category, and the word 'children' is a hyperlink. If I click that, it takes me to the children category page:

Gift ideas for children

Posted on July 3, 2013

These are gift ideas for children. These are gift ideas for children. These are gift ideas for children. These are gift ideas for children. These are gift ideas for children. These are gift ideas for children. These are gift ideas for children. These are gift ideas for children. These are gift ideas for children.

These are gift ideas for children. These are gift ideas for children. These are gift ideas for children. These are gift ideas for children. These are gift ideas for children. These are gift ideas for children.

These are gift ideas for children. These are gift ideas for children. These are gift ideas for children. These are gift ideas for children. These are gift ideas for children. These are gift ideas for children. These are gift ideas for children. These are gift ideas for children. These are gift ideas for children. These are gift ideas for children. These are gift ideas for children.

These are gift ideas for children. These are gift ideas for children. These are gift ideas for

That page also contains the full post.

The duplication doesn't stop there. WordPress has also created an author page. If I go to the author page:

Gift ideas for children

Posted on July 3, 2013

These are gift ideas for children. These are gift ideas for children. These are gift ideas for children. These are gift ideas for children. These are gift ideas for children. These are gift ideas for children. These are gift ideas for children. These are gift ideas for children. These are gift ideas for children.

These are gift ideas for children. These are gift ideas for children. These are gift ideas for children. These are gift ideas for children. These are gift ideas for children. These are gift ideas for children. These are gift ideas for children.

These are gift ideas for children. These are gift ideas for children. These are gift ideas for children. These are gift ideas for children. These are gift ideas for children. These are gift ideas for children. These are gift ideas for children. These are gift ideas for children. These are gift ideas for children. These

Once again, we have yet another duplicated copy of the same article.

But wait, there's more! What if I added a few tags to the post? Here I've added four tags to this demo article:

The tags are boys, girls, over 10 & under 12. These are supposed to help classify the gift ideas. However, WordPress creates a page for each of these tags, and guess what?

I'll give you a clue by showing you one of the four tag pages:

Gift ideas for children

Posted on July 3, 2013

These are gift ideas for children. These are gift ideas for children. These are gift ideas for children. These are gift ideas for children. These are gift ideas for children. These are gift ideas for children. These are gift ideas for children. These are gift ideas for children. These are gift ideas for children.

These are gift ideas for children. These are gift ideas for children. These are gift ideas for children. These are gift ideas for children. These are gift ideas for children. These are gift ideas for children.

Yes, that's right. The full article is published on each of the four tag pages too.

So how many times does this one post appear on the site? Well assuming I haven't missed one or two copies (something which is quite possible), we have the following:

Homepage, post page, category page, date archive, author page, and four tag pages. That's nine copies of the exact same article. And that happens with every article you publish on your site.

Now, do you see why WordPress desperately needs to be SEO'd? This type of duplication can kill your rankings in Google.

If you are starting to have palpitations, thinking you have made the wrong decision choosing WordPress, relax. I'll walk you through it step by step. It really isn't so difficult to solve these problems once you know how.

10. Menus & Site Navigation

Visitors like a site with good navigation and Google likes a site that keeps its visitors happy. Of course, there is more to it than that. Good navigation on a site will help the search engines find, and even categorize your content.

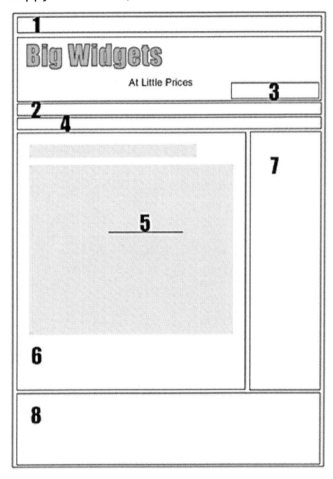

On a website, there are various places where navigation can appear. These typically include:

1.   A menu above the site logo.

2.   A menu below the site logo.

3.   A search box in the same area as the site logo, often off to the right.

4.   Breadcrumb navigation underneath the page header, but above the web page opening header.

5.   Links to other pages within the body of the content, as in-context links.

6.   After the content of the page, maybe as a 'related articles' or 'You may also be interested in these' types of link lists.

7. A menu in the left and/or right sidebar.

8. A menu in the page footer.

Where you insert your navigation may be determined by your choice of WordPress template. For example, some templates offer positions 1 or 2, but not both. Others offer both positions. And some may offer two navigation menus in position 2, but none in position 1.

As for the search box, this can appear in the logo area, or in the sidebar. I've even seen them in page footers. Therefore, this diagram is only a rough guide.

Before we look at how to create the various forms of navigation in WordPress, let me mention one thing. Create your navigation for human visitors, not search engines. That means using the most logical and aesthetically pleasing links in the menu. Do not, under any circumstances, stuff keywords into your navigation menus and links.

For example, if you had a website about prom dresses, and had sections on your site to various brands of prom dress, you might be tempted to use something like:

- ☐ PacificPlex Prom Dresses
- ☐ Ever-Pretty Prom Dresses
- ☐ Moonar Prom Dresses
- ☐ Hot from Hollywood Prom Dresses
- ☐ US Fairytailes Prom Dresses

Notice the repetition of the words 'Prom Dresses'. Why do you think some webmasters do this? Is it to help their visitors? Well, considering the whole site is about prom dresses, I'd assume not. This is done purely for the search engines for two reasons:

1. In this menu, the phrase 'prom dresses' appears five times in the hope that the page would rank better for that term. In the good old days of pre-2011 SEO, this would have worked. Today it's more likely to get you a Penguin penalty.

2. Each item in the menu will link to a page on the site. That link uses anchor text (the text you as the visitor see for any given link). In this type of menu, the keyword-stuffed anchor text is there as an attempt to boost the rankings of the page the link points to for its anchor text phrase. Say if this site had 100 pages, each using the same prom dress menu. This means each of the five pages in the menu would have 100 links pointing to them. That's 100 of the exact same anchor texts. Again, pre-2011, this worked. Today it does not, and this tactic will come back to bite you (or do Penguins nip?).

TIP: Look at the 'SEO' on your site. If you cannot say with 100% that you have done it in your visitor's best interests, then get rid of it. This goes for site navigation, content, and internal linking between pages, etc.

OK, with that said, how do you implement navigation into WordPress?

Well, there are a number of different ways.

You can use plugins. You can also use the menu system built into WordPress.

In many cases, you will know exactly which links you want in a navigation area. These links are usually fixed and rarely change. In this instance, I recommend you use the menu system built into WordPress.

On other occasions, you might want a list of the most recent posts, or posts related specifically to the current one. These menus are constantly changing as new content gets added to the site, and are therefore best handled with plugins.

10.1. Recommended Navigation

Let me make the recommendations first, and then I'll show you how to implement them.

To start off (you can add or change this later), I suggest that you have the following four navigation features:

1. **A "legal" menu:** Either above or below the site logo or in the footer, where there are links to your 'legal pages'. That's the Contact, Privacy, Disclaimers, and so forth. These links should be 'nofollowed', and the actual legal pages should be set to 'noindex', 'Follow' and 'No Archive'. This menu should also have a dofollow link to the "About Us" page, which is often one of the most visited pages on a website.

2. **A search box:** If your theme supports a search box in the header area, you might want it there. However, I personally prefer a search box at the top of the sidebar (right or left, whichever I use).

3. **A main navigation menu:** In the logo area or sidebar (right or left), that links to the main sections of your website (the main categories and/or most important pages).

4. **Sidebar dynamic menus:** Each category (or main section) of your site should have a different navigation menu in the sidebar. Google likes dynamic menus that change depending on where a visitor is. For example, if you are in the mountain bike section of a site, the main navigation menu should be related to mountain bikes. If you are in the road bike section, the main navigation menu relates to road bikes.

Personally, the type of sites I build also benefit from a 'related posts' section, either after the main content of a post or in the sidebar (done using the YARPP' plugin). However, it depends on the type of site you build, so this may not suit your particular project. I also implement internal linking between the posts on the site using context-sensitive links (this is done using the 'C.I. Backlinks' plugin). The internal linking of posts on a site is something that most of the big players do (see Wikipedia for example), and it really does help your pages get indexed and rank better.

10.2. Implementing the Four Main Navigation Features

Let's look at the 'legal menu' first.

10.2.1. Implementing Legal Menus

If you log in to the Dashboard and go to Appearance -> Menus, you'll be able to create a menu that contains links to your legal pages.

I always give menus a name that will explain what the menu is for, so in this case, I'd call it "legal".

You do need to make some of the links in this menu "nofollow", so let me show you how to do that.

Pull down the Screen Options (top right of the Dashboard), and make sure that '**Link Relationship (XFN)**' is checked.

You can now expand the items in your menu:

Type the word **nofollow** into the link relationship box.

Repeat this for all your legal pages, and don't forget to save your menu.

Once you have the menu saved, you can then insert it into your theme. At the top of the screen, you should see the **Manage Locations** tab:

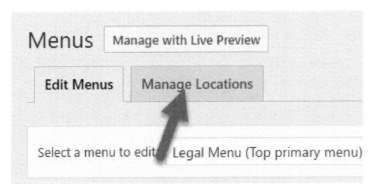

Click on that to open up the locations screen. What you'll see depends on the theme you are using. The following is for the Twenty Fourteen theme:

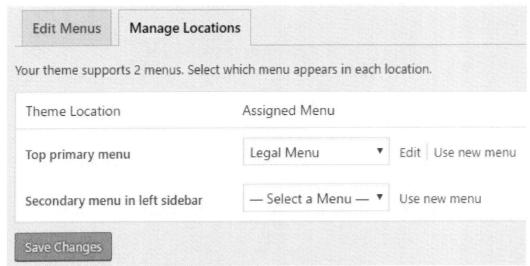

You can see that this theme has two areas allocated for menus. The **top primary menu** and the **secondary menu in the left sidebar**. You can use the drop-down boxes to select a menu for each location. If you are unsure where on your site one of these locations is found, add a menu and visit the site. You'll see where the menu has been added.

Here is another theme:

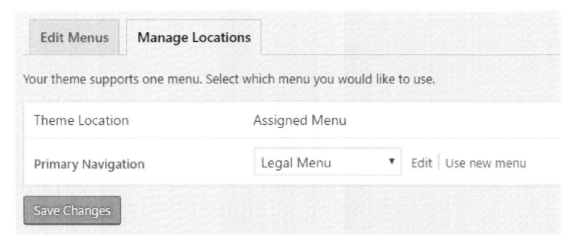

This one only allocates one area for a menu. You can easily add a menu to the sidebar of any theme using a Custom Menu widget, so it's not absolutely necessary that your theme offers this location by default.

If you have specific requirements for your menu locations, you should check how many menus (and where they are inserted) your theme offers before you decide which theme to use for your site.

OK, so how do you add the menu to the footer?

With some themes, this is very easy.

Go to the Appearance -> Widgets screen.

On the right of the screen, you will see the areas that can accept widgets. For example, the Twenty Seventeen theme offers me three locations for widgets:

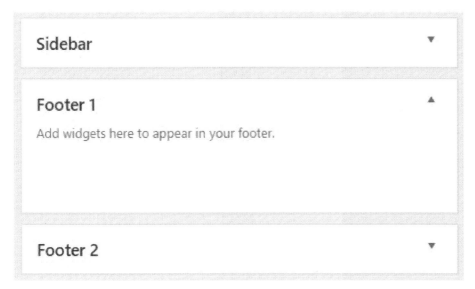

The sidebar and two footers. If your theme has two footer areas, one is likely to be the left half of the footer and one the right half. Some themes offer three footer widgets, so the footer is split into equal thirds.

On the left, you should be able to see the Custom Menu widget.

Simply drag the Custom Menu Widget into the Footer Widget area (or sidebar if that is where you want your menu), and then select the legal menu:

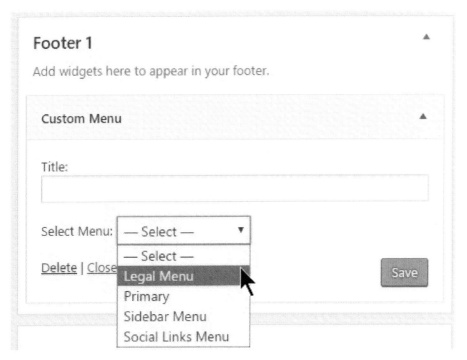

Congratulations, you've just added your legal menu to the footer area of your site. Go and check it out.

All links will be nofollow because we set that up in the actual menu settings.

There is one other task we need to do. That is to make sure our legal pages are set up so that they are 'noindex', 'Follow', and 'No Archive'. Fortunately, this is easy with the Yoast SEO plugin we installed earlier.

Go to each of your legal pages in turn and open them in the editor (Pages -> All Pages, then click on the title of the page in the list).

The Yoast SEO plugin has added a section to all post/page edit screens. It's labeled as **Yoast SEO** and it has three vertical tabs:

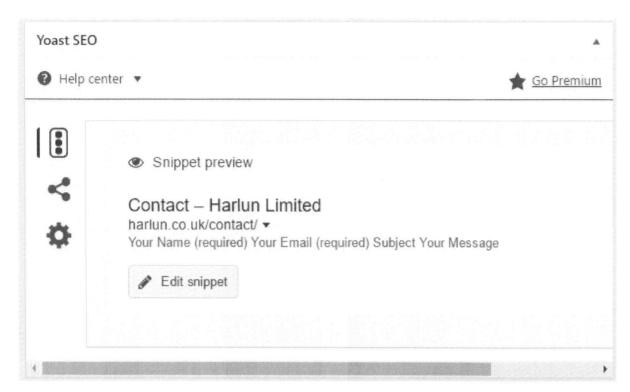

If you don't see this, make sure the Yoast SEO box is checked in the **Screen Options**.

We want to select the bottom tab (the cog):

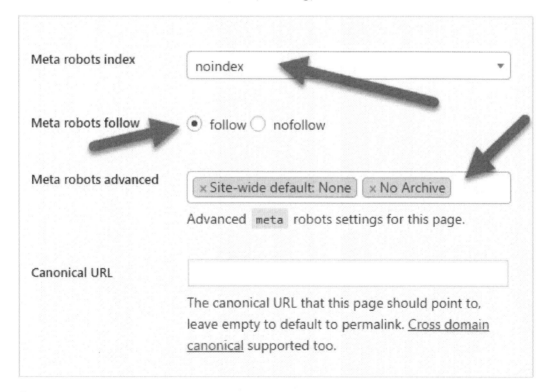

Select 'noindex' from the drop-down box at the top, 'Follow' from the radio button, and click into the Meta robots advanced box, and select 'No Archive' from the list box.

Now click the page's 'Update' button to save the changes.

Repeat this procedure for all other legal pages (and pages/posts that you don't want to appear in the search engines).

OK, now you have a legal menu on your site, with links set as nofollow, and the pages themselves set as noindex. These two settings will prevent Google from indexing pages that are not important to your site, and thus stop valuable Page Rank from flowing to these pages, meaning more link juice for your important content.

10.2.2. Implementing a Search Box

WordPress comes with a search widget, so you can start off by using that. They aren't actually very good, so I recommend you eventually switch to using a Google custom search (search Google for instructions when you are ready), but the WordPress search feature will do to get you started.

Simply drag the 'Search' widget to the widgetized area where you want it to. Some themes will offer you a 'Header Right' option. This will insert a widget into the right-hand side of the logo area. You can drag the search box widget there if you want to. Alternatively, drag it to the top of the main or primary sidebar.

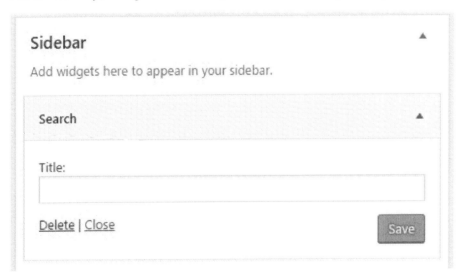

You can enter a title for the widget if you like. The title will then appear right above the search box. However, the title isn't really necessary. Here is a search box inserted into my sidebar in the Twenty Seventeen theme without a title:

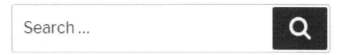

It looks great as it is!

10.2.3. Main Site Navigation Menu

The main site navigation should link to the main areas of your site (categories). These links should all be dofollow to help spread link juice around the site.

If you don't want to use the default menu locations for your main site navigation, you can insert that into the sidebar if you wish. Drag and drop a '**Custom Menu**' widget into the area you want your main navigation to appear, and select your main site menu. However, I do think the best option for main site navigation is across the top of your site, just under the logo, so I recommend you insert it there if your theme allows.

10.2.4. Dynamic Navigation Menus

The last type of navigation I suggested you use is dynamic navigation. These are menus that change depending on the area of the site a visitor is reading. We used the example of a bike website earlier. If someone is browsing the mountain bike section, the "dynamic" menu should show further options related to mountain bikes. When reading content on road bikes, the dynamic menus should offer further road bike content. After all, if someone wants to switch from mountain bikes to road bikes, the main navigation at the top will allow them to do that.

To achieve dynamic menus, we need the '**Dynamic Widgets**' plugin that I recommended earlier. When this is installed, EVERY widget you add in the Appearance -> Widgets section of the dashboard has a new feature:

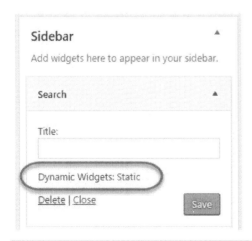

See the **Dynamic Widgets: Static**?

That word 'Static' is a hyperlink that takes you to the settings for the widget. Click on it and you get to specify exactly where on the site you want the widget to appear.

The default setting is 'Static', which means the widget appears on every page & post of the entire site, but you can change the default. Say you have a custom menu that you only want appearing on the homepage.

Click on the "static" link to be taken to the configuration screen.

This opens up a large page of options.

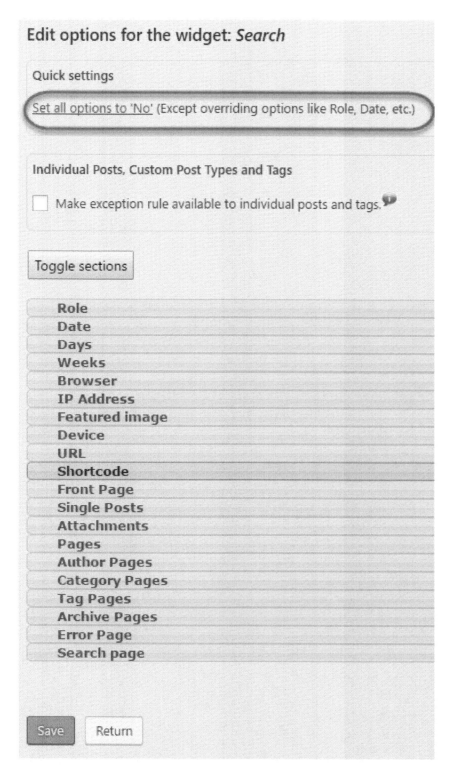

Each of these 'horizontal bars' will open up if you click on them.

Since we only want the menu to appear on the homepage, the first thing we need to do is click the link at the top of these options: **Set all options to 'No'**.

If we now click on any one of these bars, it will expand, showing us that it is set to 'No'.

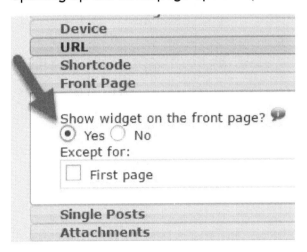

This means the widget will not appear anywhere on the site. We need to fix this by opening up the homepage options (called 'Front Page' in this plugin), and select **'Yes'**.

Now, don't forget to save the settings by clicking the **'Save'** button at the bottom. This will then return you to the widgets area of the Dashboard.

If you look at the Custom Menu widget, you'll see that additional information I told you about is now listed in the Dynamic Widgets section:

Dynamic Widgets: Dynamic

Options set for Archive Pages, Attachments, Author Pages, Category Pages, Error Page, Pages, Search page, Single Posts and Tag Pages.

Delete | Close   Save

The word 'Static' now reads 'Dynamic', and we can see that the options have been set for various pages on the site.

If you check your site, you will find the main navigation menu only appears on the homepage.

To create dynamic menus for each specific area of your site, you need to set up the menu in the Appearance -> Menu section.

For example, if you have five categories on your site, set up five Custom Menus, and include the most relevant menu items for each category.

Next, add all of these custom menus to the sidebar, and then go into them, one by one, and change the settings for where they should appear on your site.

Let's assume I want the custom menu to appear only in the '**Hot from Hollywood**' category (that's the category page plus any posts in that category).

Step one will be to click the link to set all options to 'No', just as we did for the homepage. Next, we need to change two settings.

The first is in the '**Category Pages**' settings:

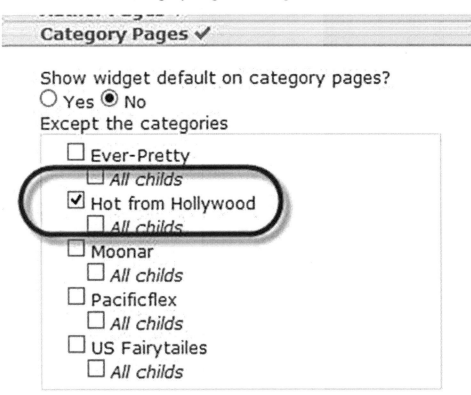

Select '**No**' at the top, and then check the '**Hot from Hollywood**' checkbox. This may sound counter-intuitive, but read the information on the plugin settings screen. We are checking the Hot from Hollywood category so that it will be the exception. We don't want the widget to appear on category pages EXCEPT for the one(s) that are checked.

OK, once saved, that will show the menu on the 'Hot from Hollywood' category page. We also need to make it appear on the posts within that category, so we have to set the '**Single Posts**' options.

Single Posts ✔

Show widget default on single posts? 💬
○ Yes ◉ No

Except the author(s)
☐ Maria

Except the categories
☐ Ever-Pretty
  ☐ *All childs*
☑ Hot from Hollywood
  ☑ *All childs*
☐ Moorlai
  ☐ *All childs*
☐ Pacificflex
  ☐ *All childs*
☐ US Fairytailes
  ☐ *All childs*

Again, we select '**No**' at the top because we don't want this widget appearing on posts, except the ones we check

The 'Hot from Hollywood' category is selected, but you also have the option to check '*All childs*', which will mean any 'Hot from Hollywood' sub-categories will also have this menu.

OK, once done, save your changes.

The menu will only appear on the 'Hot from Hollywood' category page AND all the posts within that category.

Repeat this process for each dynamic menu you are creating for your website.

I recommend you read the documentation for the dynamic widgets plugin and play around with it. As you explore the other settings, you will discover it offers an enormous level of control over widget placement on your site.

Using the techniques shown in this chapter, you can easily create custom sidebars and custom footers with any type of widget in any area that is widgetized.

This is the easiest way to create dynamic navigation systems on your website. Don't forget, besides navigation systems, you can also serve up custom adverts, custom subscription boxes, custom videos, etc., and all on different sections of the site.

11. Comment System

The comment systems and how to integrate them into your site is an important, yet often over-looked piece of the on-site SEO puzzle.

The comments on your site are VERY important. A lot of comments tell visitors that your site is busy. If it's busy, then it's likely to be trusted by more people. If it's trusted, it will do better in Google too.

However, all of this is dependent on having good quality comments. Comments need to add to the 'conversation' that has gone before them. Put more specifically, do the comments add to the original article, either by way of an opinion, additional information, or a question? Another good type of comment is when a visitor replies to someone else's remarks, but again, only if those replies are adding to the conversation. These are the types of comments you need to try and get on your site.

When a website is new, it's all too easy to approve poor comments just to make the site look visited. Don't do it! Never approve a comment *unless* it actually adds something to the post topic and conversation already on-going, that's if there are other comments of course.

Typical comments you should NOT approve include the congratulatory comments, like "Well done!", or "Great post". Even "Thanks for writing about this topic in a way I can understand". Although the latter might sound sincere, it adds absolutely nothing to the conversation because there is no reference to the topic in question.

Get used to approving only the best comments. Even if you don't get very many to begin with (which is quite possible), great comments add value to the overall visitor experience of your website. Or to put it another way, a website full of poor & spammy comments will put your visitors off and they won't have much confidence in you or the credibility of your site.

12. RSS Feeds

WordPress automatically creates several RSS feeds for your site.

You can access the main feed for your site by adding **/feed** to the end of your domain URL.

The feed for my SEO website is **ezSEONews.com/feed**.

We set up the RSS feed earlier to show just 10 posts and only the title and excerpts of those. Therefore, the main feed will show the last 10 posts you published on your site.

WordPress also creates six other feeds:

1. Comments – this feed shows the last 10 comments made on your site.
2. Post-specific feeds – which show the last 10 comments made on a particular post.
3. Category feeds – which show the last 10 posts made in a particular category.
4. Tag feeds – which show the last 10 posts using a particular tag.
5. Author feeds – showing the last 10 posts made by a particular author.
6. Search feeds – showing the search results for a particular keyword phrase.

I won't go into details showing you how to find all of these feeds. If you are interested, you can read the WordPress codex article on this topic:

http://codex.wordpress.org/WordPress_Feeds

From an SEO point of view, feeds are interesting. For example, there are a number of RSS feed submission services where you can get backlinks to your site by submitting your feed(s). Whenever you add fresh content, these feeds get updated, linking back to the new page. In terms of helping pages rank higher, these types of links won't help at all, but they can get your new content indexed a lot quicker. What I would suggest here is not to overdo this type of submission. Pick maybe one or two of the top RSS feed sites, and submit your main site feed to each.

One thing I like to use feeds for is adding a recent posts section to my site's sidebar, or footer. WordPress comes with an RSS widget, and all you need to do is supply the feed URL for it to work.

For example, on my SEO site, I have a category on Kindle Publishing. I can grab the feed URL for that category:

http://ezseonews.com/seo/kindle-publishing/feed/

I then add it to an RSS widget:

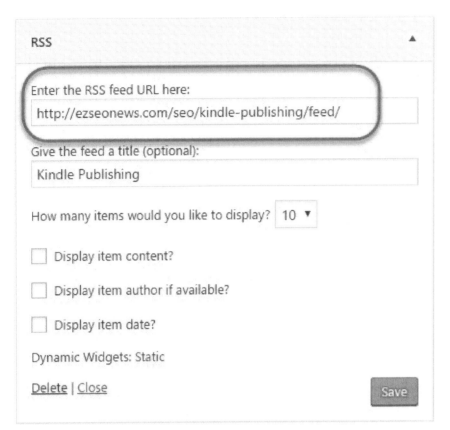

If I only want the feed to appear on certain areas of the site, I can set this up using the dynamic widget options. For example, I might only want this widget showing in the "publishing" area of my website. That would be easy to implement by setting the dynamic options. The widget would then display the 10 most recent posts from that section in my sidebar.

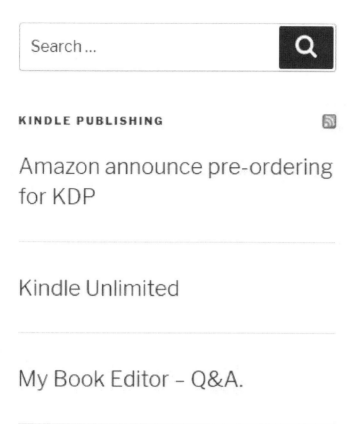

Search...

KINDLE PUBLISHING

Amazon announce pre-ordering for KDP

Kindle Unlimited

My Book Editor – Q&A.

Best of all is that as new content is added to the site, the feed is updated, and so is the list in my sidebar.

This has a couple of benefits:

1. You can highlight other recent articles in a given category. If someone is reading an article about one aspect of Kindle publishing, the chances are these other articles will be of interest too.

2. From an SEO perspective, this is good because you have inter-linking of the Kindle publishing articles, each reinforcing the theme of your pages and providing spiderable links to the other articles in the 'silo'.

13. Google Authorship & WordPress User Profiles

Google is always updating its algorithm. There are hundreds of minor updates every year, with some major ones sprinkled in between. In the last couple of years, we've had to contend with Panda, Penguin and then Penguin 2.0 (which was a major upgrade to the original). All of these updates have been necessary because Google has faced a constant battle with webmasters trying to game the system; that is webmasters who want their content to rank #1 in the Google search results pages.

We all want to be ranked #1 for various search phrases - obviously - but we don't all deserve these top slot(s). Google has a problem with webmasters that try to force their content to the top of the first page. Google wants total control. They need to be able to decide which content deserves to be at the top, and not leave that up to webmasters, who can and do, try all manner of techniques to get these valuable positions.

One of the most abused SEO techniques over the years has been link building. The general principle has always been more is better. Webmasters have always considered link building to be a safe practice because you cannot control who links to your site. Google themselves even told us once that links could not hurt a site's rankings.

I guess the search giant finally snapped, because today, bad links can cause you ranking problems. To help webmasters fix link problems, Google introduced the disavow tool. You can use this to list those links pointing at your site which you do not approve of. This now means that site owners have full control over the links to their pages, signifying Google have shifted the responsibility of bad links away from their algorithm, and onto the webmaster. In other words, if you have bad links pointing to your site, it is *your* fault as far as Google is concerned.

While the Google vs. Webmasters battle has raged on all these years, Google has been constantly looking for other 'signals' they could use to help them better rank web pages. The holy grail of 'signals' would be one that webmasters could not manipulate to their advantage.

13.1. Google Authorship

Google introduced 'Google Authorship' as a way to connect a piece of content with its true author. Unfortunately, Google stopped their "authorship program" in the last couple of years, so it's no longer an option. It was great while it lasted because once set up, Google would instantly know you were the true author of content as you posted it on your site. That meant content thieves we left out in the cold.

I'm not sure why Google stopped using authorship, but I do think you need to take all the measures you can to be credited as the true author of your own site content. For that reason, I want to talk a little bit about Gravatars and author biographies.

13.2. Gravatars & the Author Bio on Your Site

Everyone likes to see who they are dealing with and in the more anonymous online world, it helps build your brand. Putting a face behind the name adds trust and credibility to your site(s) too. I, therefore, recommend you use a real photo of yourself and include it in an "author bio" after every post on your site. You should use the same photo when you leave comments on other websites, too.

The first step in achieving this is to sign up for a Gravatar:

https://en.gravatar.com/

When you get there, you'll see a button to "Create your own Gravatar". Click on that and follow the instructions. Gravatars are closely linked to an email address. When you leave a comment on another website, that website will check to see if the email address used in the comment has an associated Gravatar. If it is, that Gravatar image will be used with your comment.

Therefore, you need to enter the *exact* same email address that you've set up in your Wordpress Dashboard.

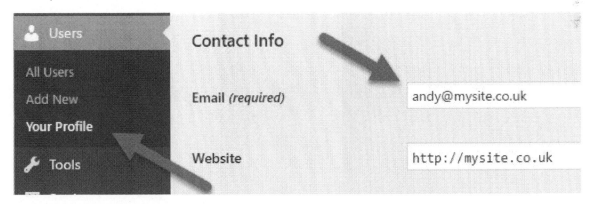

Just follow the on-screen instructions to set up your Gravatar.

Once your account has been set up, you can upload an image and connect your email address to that photo. Try to use this same photo of yourself in all promotional activity. This will help brand you as the expert wherever you contribute, and people will start to recognize your face.

NOTE: You can add multiple email addresses to your Gravatar account, so if you control lots of sites, or have many email addresses, you can assign the same (or a different), image to every email you'd like a Gravatar for.

Once this is set up, if you leave comments on blogs that have Gravatars enabled (btw, most of them do), then your image will show up next to your comments (assuming you entered the same email address when submitting them). Some forums also use Gravatars for images, so as you can see, we have multiple ways to brand ourselves and build trust around the web.

13.2.1. Author Bio Boxes

To set up the author bio on your posts, login to the dashboard and go to the Users -> Your profile page.

About Yourself

Biographical Info

I am a Science teacher by training, but have been working online for over a decade, specializing in search engine optimization and affiliate marketing. I publish a free weekly <a href="http://ezseonews.com/">Internet Marketing newsletter</a> with tips, advice, tutorials, and more.
You can subscribe to my free daily paper called the <a href="http://paper.li/ezSEONews/1320871114">Google Daily</a> and follow me on <a href="https://www.facebook.com/ezSEONewsletter">Facebook</a> or<a href="https://twitter.com/ezseonews">Twitter</a>. I am also on <a href="https://plus.google.com/107232271221234192246/posts">Google + </a>

Share a little biographical information to fill out your profile. This may be shown publicly.

Profile Picture

You can change your profile picture on Gravatar.

Under profile picture, you should see your Gravatar!

In the '**Biographical info**' box, enter the bio that you want to appear for each post on your site.

If your theme inserts an author bio box after posts, this should then appear after each post like this:

About Andy Williams

I am a Science teacher by training, but have been working online for over a decade, specializing in search engine optimization and affiliate marketing. I publish a free weekly Internet Marketing newsletter with tips, advice, tutorials, and more. You can subscribe to my free daily paper called the Google Daily and follow me on Facebook or Twitter. I am also on Google +

View all posts by Andy Williams →

If your theme does not natively support author bio boxes, then you can add these using a plugin instead. Search the plugin repository for "author bio box" and there will be a number you can try. For example, this one:

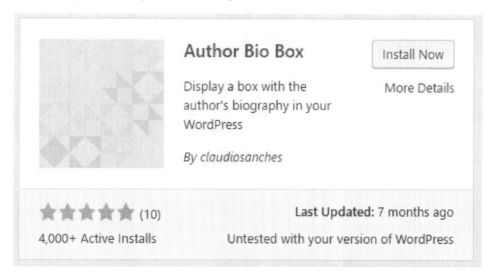

I set this plugin up with my information on a site using the Twenty Seventeen (which does not natively add an author bio box after posts). This is the result:

Andy Williams

I am a Science teacher by training, but have been working online for over a decade, specializing in search engine optimization and affiliate marketing. I publish a free weekly Internet Marketing newsletter with tips, advice, tutorials, and more. You can subscribe to my free daily paper called the Google Daily and follow me on Facebook or Twitter. I am also on Google +

That's not bad at all!

14. Robots.txt File

The robots.txt file is a plain text file that contains various instructions for the search engines and other bots visiting your site. It includes details on specific folders and files that the search engines should, or should not spider.

For example, you could tell the search engines to ignore all files within a specific folder on your server.

A few years ago, a good robots.txt file was important for a Wordpress site, and Google expected one. Today, Google says you can use one if you want, but it prefers you don't. To properly spider and index a Wordpress website, Google needs access to most folders and files on your server.

Therefore, I recommend you don't bother with a robots.txt file. In fact, the only reason I am including a section on the robots.txt file in this book is because I get asked about it so often by my Wordpress students.

15. WWW or No WWW?

Some websites use the 'www.' prefix and others don't. Google actually treats these as different URLs, so www.mysite.com is different to mysite.com. It really doesn't matter whether you choose www or non-www, but it is vital you are consistent. All links on your site or pointing to your site MUST use the same version.

You, therefore, need to decide which way you want your site's URL to be displayed.

Once WordPress is installed, visit your homepage by typing in the www. version of the domain. See what WordPress does by default. More often than not, you URL will be re-directed to the non-WWW version of the web page.

My advice is to use whatever WordPress shows you by default unless you have a good reason to want the other version.

Once decided on your preferred version, login to your WordPress Dashboard and go to the Settings -> General screen

WordPress Address (URL)	http://ezseonews.com
Site Address (URL)	http://ezseonews.com

Enter the address here if you want your site homepage to b

You should see that version in the Wordpress Address (URL) and the Site Address (URL).

Now you need to tell Google which version you want to use. You can do this in Google Search Console, so log in to your GSC account, and click on the site you are working on.

Now click on the cog icon located in the top-right, and select '**Site Settings**'.

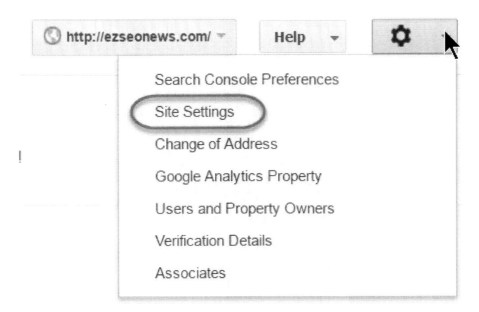

In the screen that loads, you can select the correct version of your site by selecting the **'Preferred domain'** radio button:

Site Settings

Make sure you save your settings. OK, you are done with this section.

16. Pages Versus Posts

While I cover this in more detail in Wordpress books and courses, it is important you understand the basics, so I'll go over fundamentals again here.

One of the things that many WordPress beginners get confused about is the difference between WordPress Pages and WordPress Posts. What makes things even more confusing is the tendency to call any web page a 'page', even if it is actually a 'post'.

To try to make things clearer, when I am referring to a web page loaded in your browser, whether it's been created as a WordPress post or a WordPress page, I'll call it a web page. If I am specifically talking about a WordPress post or a WordPress page, then I'll make sure I prefix the words post and page with 'WordPress'.

Here is a quick key:

Web page: Any web page that's loaded in your internet browser.

WordPress Page: Content created as a WordPress 'Page'.

WordPress Post: Content created as a WordPress 'Post'.

Got it?

OK, let's carry on.

With WordPress, we need to make the distinction between WordPress pages and WordPress posts, as they are both different and have distinctive purposes.

Let's look at the features of these two:

16.1. Posts

- Can be displayed chronologically or in reverse chronological order in a number of places on your site, including author pages, category pages, most recent posts, and RSS feeds.

- They are assigned to categories.

- They can be tagged.

- Posts can allow visitor comments.

- Posts appear in your site's RSS feeds and can, therefore, be syndicated to email subscribers if using a service like FeedBurner.

- Posts can have excerpts, which is basically a short summary of the written piece. These can be used by WordPress and plugins to supply a Meta Description tag, and short descriptions of posts in related posts features, etc.

- Posts do not have a custom template feature. There was a feature introduced in WordPress 3.1 called 'Post Formats'. Not all themes support these, but they are available to all theme developers if they wish to use them. Basically, this feature allows posts to be classified as *standard, aside, audio, chat, gallery, link, quote, status* or *video*, and their appearance changes depending on the post format. You can read more about post format here: http://codex.wordpress.org/Post_Formats

16.2. Pages

- These are 'static' and not listed or sorted by date order. They are, however, hierarchical, so you can have a parent page with several child pages.

- Pages are not put into categories.

- Pages do not have tags.

- Although it is possible to enable comments on pages, this isn't typically something you want to do.

- Pages do not appear in your site's RSS feed and are therefore not syndicated to email subscribers when using FeedBurner.

- Pages do not have excerpts.

- Pages can use a 'custom template' feature making it possible to vary the appearance of them (read your template documentation to see what is available).

- You can set up a WordPress page to be used as your homepage.

16.3. When to Use WordPress Pages and WordPress Posts

As you can see, there are several distinct differences between the two.

In terms of SEO, Google doesn't care whether a web page is created as a WordPress page or a WordPress post. However, the features we have available with WordPress posts make them the obvious choice for content that we hope to rank well for in the SERPs. Because of this, I recommend you use WordPress pages and WordPress posts as follows:

Use WordPress pages for the 'legal pages' (disclaimers, privacy statement, contact, about us, etc), and use WordPress posts for everything else.

When I say everything else, I am referring to all content that is written to engage the visitor. If it's something you want a visitor to read, and maybe comment on or share to their own social circles, definitely use a post.

By sticking to this simple rule, you can take advantage of the way WordPress was designed to work, and thus get maximum SEO benefits out of it.

The only exception I make to this rule is when I want to set up my homepage using a WordPress page, rather than one which displays the last 10 WordPress posts (more on this in the next chapter).

17. Setting up the Homepage

There are two main ways of setting up a homepage in WordPress. You can either create a WordPress page for it, or you can base your homepage to display the latest WordPress posts.

You make that decision in the **Settings -> Reading** options.

Essentially, using a WordPress page (the static page option in the screenshot) for your homepage means you can have a more 'static' front page, i.e., one that doesn't change too much.

If you choose to go with the 'latest posts' option for your homepage (as is typical for blogs), then it will always be changing, showing your very latest post at the top of it.

For most themes, if you choose a static page for your homepage, you simply select the page that you want to use for your homepage and you are done. That Wordpress page will be displayed as your homepage content.

However, not all Wordpress themes are the same.

WordPress themes have evolved and one of my favorite features of the Genesis theme is the way it handles the homepage. The Genesis framework was the first template system I found that allowed us to create a homepage using widgets. You should be familiar with widgets by now, but if not, just think of them as user-definable areas where you can insert whatever you want.

The Genesis child themes do differ in the number and location of widgetized areas on the homepage, so you would need to check them out before buying one.

For example, the Genesis Lifestyle theme gives you three widgetized areas in addition to the usual header, sidebars, and footers. You have 'Home', 'Home left' and 'Home right' and these are positioned directly where the main content of the homepage will go.

Here are those three widget areas:

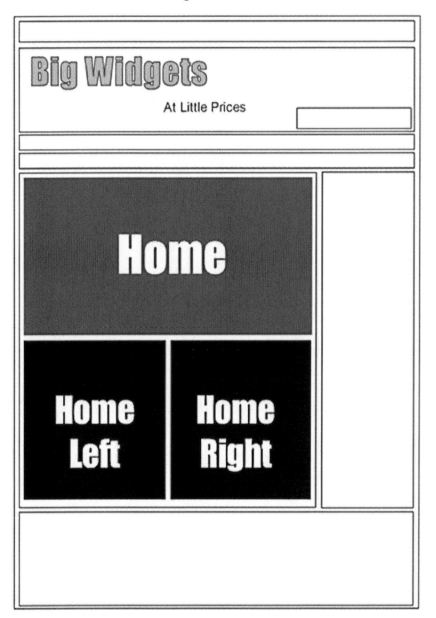

Those three widget areas can contain posts, pages, or just about anything else.

You can see this theme in action on the Lifestyle demo theme site:

http://demo.studiopress.com/lifestyle/

By contrast, the Genesis Balance theme has two homepage widget areas called 'Home Featured Left' and 'Home Featured Right'.

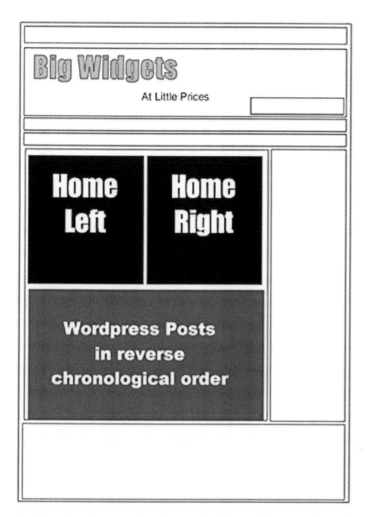

Under the 'home featured left' and 'home featured right' areas of the homepage, the normal WordPress loop is used to show the latest posts in reverse chronological order.

I love the Genesis child themes because they give me so much scope for designing a homepage the way I want it to appear. The idea of using widgets for the homepage, wherever it came from, is pure genius.

Check out all of the Genesis themes here:

http://ezseonews.com/genesis

18. Site-Wide Considerations

There are a couple of things that you should be implementing on a site-wide scale.

18.1. "Nofollow" Links

This is a concern for all posts and pages on your entire site.

The nofollow tag can be added to any link to stop the search engines from following it.

Here is an example link with the nofollow attribute assigned to it:

\<a href="http://google.com" **rel="nofollow"**\>Google\</a\>

It's a good idea to nofollow links on your site that you don't want to waste link juice on. These include the legal pages (contact, privacy, etc). We've already seen this earlier in the book when we set up the legal menu to automatically nofollow the links.

I'd also recommend you nofollow *all* affiliate links.

When you are writing content that links to another authority website, do NOT add nofollow. We want Google to know we endorse these other credible sites by leaving the nofollow off the link.

These guidelines go for all pages on your site, and not just the homepage.

18.2. Getting Social on Your Site

It is a good idea to include ways for your visitors to follow you and share your content with their followers.

We mentioned a plugin earlier called "Social Media Flying Icons". There are plenty of plugins to choose from, and it will depend on personal choice. My advice though is to find one you like and use it. Give your visitors a way to share your content with their audience, and to follow you on your social channels.

Google are certainly paying a lot more attention to social shares as ranking signals.

19. SEO When Writing Content

In this section, I just want to highlight a few points about writing content and SEO, plus mention the specific features you can use to help with the Search Engine Optimisation on your WordPress pages and WordPress posts.

With any type of content, posts or pages, it is important to follow a few general rules to ensure you do not fall foul of Google's Panda or Penguin algorithm. In the old days of SEO (pre-2011), webmasters tried to rank specifically for a keyword phrase or two, and would insert the exact phrase in a number of places like the title, filename, H1 header, opening paragraph, closing paragraph, ALT tags, and also worked into various other paragraphs within the article body too. Today that is just asking for trouble. The era of targeting specific words and phrases are just about over.

The best approach to writing good quality content is to write for your visitor and not the search engines. If you right naturally, and with a sound knowledge of the topic, you will automatically include relevant words and phrases into your content anyway, which will help it rank for a whole host of search phrases. By all means include a specific phrase somewhere, such as the title or H1 header, but don't, whatever you do, start stuffing the same phrase in as many places as possible. Google are clever enough now to know what the page is about, even without strategic keyword placements by the webmaster. Concentrate on providing great quality content that will please your visitors, and that Google will want to rank highly because it deserves to.

With that in mind, create a compelling headline for your post, and don't try to stuff it with individual keywords or keyword phrases either. Just aim to create quality content, and forget about trying to optimize it for any specific words or phrases.

Tip: If you read your content out loud, and it sounds unnatural because of keywords that have been forced into the text, then it's not great content.

Another thing to think about is the 'slug' of your post or page. The slug is the filename, and it is automatically generated by WordPress when you publish content. WordPress takes your content's title, replaces spaces with dashes, removes any non-alphanumeric characters, and uses that (see below):

In the screenshot above, the title of the article is 'curcumin for weight loss'. The slug that WordPress created is **curcumin-for-weight-loss**.

You can change the slug if you want to; perhaps if there's a better way of naming it, or maybe the title of your article is long (it's a good idea to keep your URLs short). To edit the slug, click the '**Edit**' button next to the permalink URL at the top of your post/page, and then modify it to what you want. Finally, make sure you Publish/Update your page to save the changes.

19.1. SEO for WordPress Pages

The first thing I should mention about WordPress pages is that they can now have comments. This wasn't always the case, but I guess WordPress caved in to popular demand (of those that used pages for content when they should have perhaps used posts!).

Discussion

☐ Allow comments.
☐ Allow <u>trackbacks and pingbacks</u> on this page.

NOTE: If you don't see this option on pages, check the screen options. "Discussion" needs to be checked.

The way we are using WordPress pages (for legal pages), it's unlikely you'll want to enable that option. We don't particularly want people commenting on our privacy policy or contact pages! However, if you do have a page that you would like to enable comments on, this is where you do it on a page-by-page basis (the Discussion box is located below the text editor).

Fortunately, a lot of the SEO we control on pages (and posts), is supplied to us by the Yoast SEO plugin. You'll find a section created by this plugin as you scroll down the page edit screen. It's typically located just under the text editor:

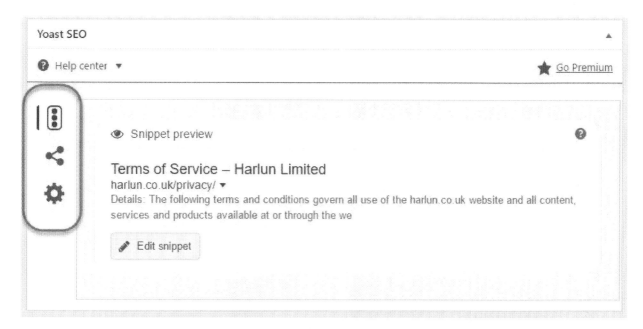

It's identical to the Yoast SEO addition on the edit posts screen we saw earlier.

There are 3 tabs down the left-hand side. The top one is the "Content Optimization" tab, which allows you to make changes to the way the page will appear in the Google search results.

If you click on Edit Snippet, you can change the title, slug and meta description shown in the snippet preview. This will affect how the page is shown in Google, allowing you to optimize titles, URL and descriptions in much the same way pay per click users have done for years to improve click through rates.

The second tab of these settings are the "Social" settings. This allows you to set a Facebook title, description, and image for the page. If someone shares the page on Facebook, these are the settings that will be used by default.

The third tab is the "Advanced" tab, offering a range of useful features.

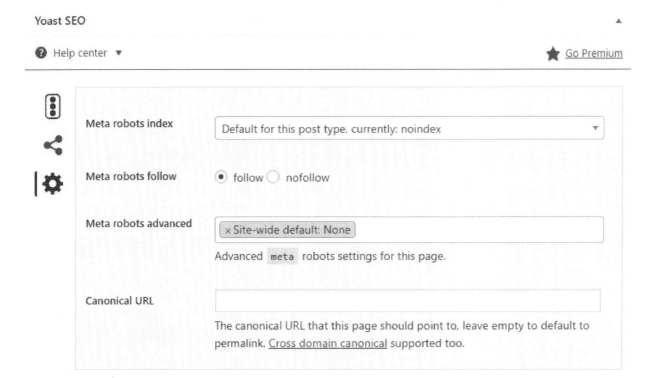

I won't go into these settings here, as we looked at them earlier in the book when setting legal pages to noindex, no archive.

OK, that's the Yoast SEO settings for WordPress pages. Let's now look at SEO on WordPress posts.

19.2. SEO for WordPress Posts

WordPress posts have a few more SEO options than WordPress pages. We still have the Yoast SEO plugin options that we saw in the previous section on 'WordPress Pages', and they are used in exactly the same way. If you need to noindex, follow a post (as we will do later when we look at setting up category pages), then you do it using the **'Advanced'** tab of that plugin's options.

Also, you will notice that if you go to **Posts -> All Posts,** in the WordPress Dashboard, there are a few extra columns tacked on to the end of the table:

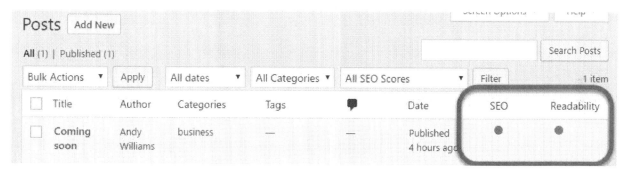

If you don't see these columns, they are probably turned off in the SEO -> Titles & Metas -> General tab of the plugin settings screen.

I would suggest you ignore these columns, as they are part of the keyword optimization features in the plugin. In fact, why not go to the settings of the plugin and turn them off:

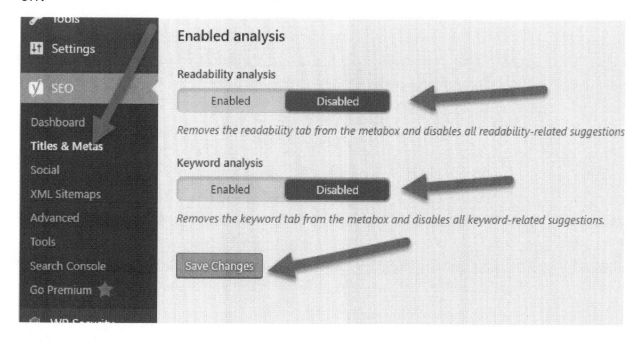

19.2.1. Post Categories

One of the benefits of using posts for publishing your main, visitor-orientated content is that you can group them into categories. These act as organized 'silos' of content, all related to the core topic. When you add a post, you can select the category from a list of those which you have already set up.

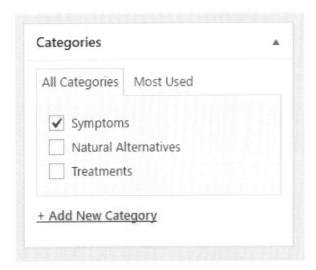

From an SEO point of view, it is better to only have posts in ONE category. If you find that you need to categorize a post into multiple categories, then you probably don't have the correct categories in the first place. Categories should be broad enough so that there isn't much, or any, overlap. If you find that you want to further classify your posts, look at using tags instead. We'll be looking more into tags later in the book.

There are a few reasons why one post for one category is a good idea.

Firstly, if you put a post in three categories, then three copies of that post will be created (one on each category page), though we will largely overcome this problem later when setting up the category pages. A more important reason for the one post one category rule is the SEO benefit. We want categories to contain tightly focused groups of content. Using a plugin like YARPP (see the plugins section of this book for details), we can set up a 'Related Posts' section for every post on the site. These related links (or excerpts with links to the related posts) show other posts within the same category. Therefore, related posts are interlinking with each other, and that will help boost your rankings. This is because Google likes it when a post has links from related content. Another SEO benefit comes from the category pages. These pages link out to highly related articles on the site, so once again, the relevancy factors of links to-and-from related content is a big on-page SEO advantage.

19.2.2. Post Tags

Tags are an additional way to categorize your content. When you add a post, you can enter one or more tags for it:

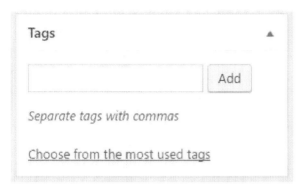

You simply enter them, with each tag separated by a comma.

For every tag you enter, WordPress creates a separate web page that lists all posts using that tag. As you can imagine, duplicate content is an issue again. When a site uses tags incorrectly, major SEO problems arise. For example, I've seen websites that have dozens of tags per post. In many cases, a tag might only be used ONCE on the entire site. That means the tag page will contain one article. What is the point of that tag page, since the article already appears on its own post web page?

The purpose of tags is similar to the purpose of categories. It's used to assemble related content into related groups so that visitors (and search engines), can find information more easily.

For example, suppose you had a website about Huskies with lots of content, videos, and photos. You could set up categories like grooming, feed, training, etc. You might also like to categorize your posts according to whether they were articles, photos or videos. You might then use the tags: articles, photos, videos. Some pieces of content would include two, or even all three of these tags, and that is fine. We do still end up with duplication issues because the same article may then be posted on two or three tag pages. However, we'll look later at how we can minimize this duplication issue and add more value to tag pages.

The benefit of the tag pages is that it adds an extra level of categorisation which the visitor will find useful (if done properly). So, someone looking for images of Huskies can visit the 'photo' tag page, and find all the pictures listed together on there. It's the same principle for those looking for videos or content, etc.

From a search engine point of view, tag pages do tend to rank well because multiple posts typically point at each tag page. Later in the book, we'll look at how we can modify these tag pages to offer our visitors, and the search engines, even more worth.

My two suggestions for using tags is to only use those that appear (or will appear), on multiple posts of the site, and that you limit the number of tags per post to a maximum of four or five.

19.2.3. Post Formatting

At the top of the WYSIWYG (What-You-See-Is-What-You-Get), editor on the edit post screen is the toolbar.

By default, the toolbar only contains the top row of buttons. To show the bottom row of tool buttons (which includes the important text formatting drop-down box), you have to click the button on the far right of the top toolbar. That button toggles between top only, and both toolbars.

Note: With formatting comes great responsibility.

With formatting options, like bold, underline & italics, only use them where you would if search engines did not exist. What I mean by that is do not be tempted to put bold or italics on the words and phrases you want to rank for. This might have worked a few years ago, but today it's a signal to Google that you are trying to over-optimise your page for those words and phrases. SEO on your page should be 'invisible', meaning it should not be obvious what you are trying to rank for when reading the content.

For headers, only include one 'Heading 1' headline per page (this uses the H1 HTML tag). Your template is likely to use an H1 for the title of the post, so you shouldn't add a second H1 header. Use headlines in hierarchies, with an H2 being the start of a new section and H3 as subsections of the H2. If you then start a new section, use another H2.

Again, as with all areas of your content, do not stuff keyword phrases into headlines because they'll do you NO favors.

19.3. Optimizing Images Used in Posts

The '**Add Media**' button above the toolbar, allows you to insert images and other media into your posts and pages. For images used in posts, I would recommend you optimize them as follows:

- Try to compress the image to as small a size as possible before uploading. Remember that when someone visits your page, the images have to download to their computers, thus slowing page load times.

- Keep image file size small, and resize images to the correct size (dimensions) before uploading. For example, if your theme content area is 600 pixels, and you want the image to take up half the width of the content, resize the image so that it is 300 pixels wide.

- Give your image a name that best describes it. Once again, remember not to keyword stuff here, and don't use words and phrases that are irrelevant to the image.

- Use ALT tags for all your images, and I say again, don't keyword stuff. Describe the image appropriately so blind or partially sighted users can understand your content.

- Consider using the Smush Image Compressions and Optimization plugin to automatically optimize images as you upload them to your website. It will also optimize images already in your media library. This optimization will make your images smaller without losing quality. Search for "smush" in the **Add New** plugins screen, and look for this one:

Install and activate the Smush Image Compression and Optimization plugin.

Once activated, you'll be taken the **WP Smush** settings (located inside the **Media** menu).

The Smush dashboard will tell you how many images need to be optimized and give you the option of "bulk smush":

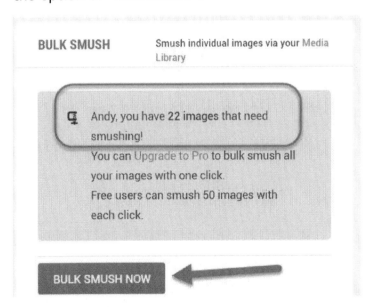

The free version does have limitations, but may be all you need. Free users can bulk smush 50 images with each click. This site of mine only has 22 images that need optimizing.

Clicking the **Bulk Smush Now** button starts the automated process.

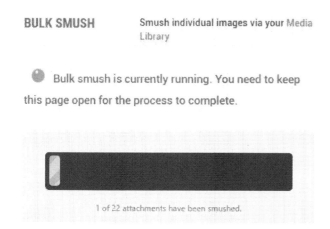

As the images are processed, the **Stats** panel will keep you updated on the progress:

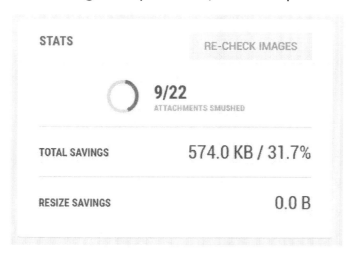

In the screenshot above, you can see 9 of the 22 images have been processed, with total savings of 574 Kb, or 31.7%.

After all 22 images were processed, Smush saved my visitors a total of 2.3MB in downloads from images:

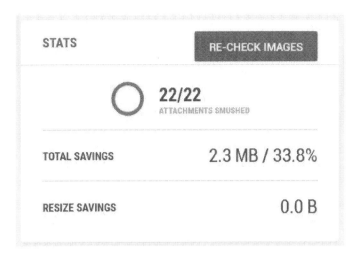

The plugin has a really cool feature. It will automatically optimize your images as you upload them. Just make sure that option is selected (it is by default):

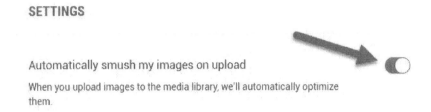

The free version of this plugin is enough for most people. However, power users may appreciate the paid features. E.g. The paid version will compress your images up to twice as much as the free version.

19.4. Internal Linking Between Posts

The YARPP plugin we mentioned in the plugins section of this book will create 'related posts' sections on each of your posts if you want them there. That helps to interlink your related content and spread link juice around your site. One of the more powerful 'on-page techniques' is to link words and phrases in one post to another 'related post', though you shouldn't do this just for the sake of internal linking.

Let me give you an example of how this is used for maximum SEO benefit.

Suppose you had an article called 'World's Best Hot Dog Recipe'. In that article, you mention a special tomato sauce that you make for your hot dogs. You have the tomato sauce recipe on your site. It makes sense to link to that tomato sauce recipe from the hot dog recipe article using an "internal link" (i.e. one that goes from one page of your site to another).

Internal linking like this is natural, helps visitors, and is a powerful SEO tool to help our pages rank better.

I did an experiment with internal linking on one of my sites. I described the experiment and results here:

http://ezseonews.com/backlinks/internal-linking-seo/

19.5. Featured Images for Posts

Posts can be assigned a featured image, which is used to show up next to the post wherever it is listed on your site. For example, here are the featured images being used in a recent posts list on one of my websites:

Recent Posts

 My Plan for 2017 - What are your plans to make sure 2 of mine.

 Ninja Outreach Review - Ninja Outreach has a suite of backlinks to your website in the way I describe in my[S Amazon). The most effective way to build backlinks in program combined with the "link bait" style content [...]

 Moving a Site from WordPress.com to WordPress.Org Wordpress.com website, but now need more power a Wordpress.com site to a Wordpress.org hosted site is

 Google's Outbound Link Penalty - Google's outbound to be affraid of.

You add featured images to a post directly in the edit post screen:

Whether you use them or not depends on how you want your site to look. Personally, I think they help break up blocks of text on a web page, therefore helping the visitor to navigate to stuff easier.

If you do use them, make sure you follow the image optimization tips above for these as well. Remember, if you have a list of say 20 posts on a category page, with 20 featured images, they are going to slow the page load time considerably. Optimizing these images as best you can, both in size (KB), and dimensions (pixels), will help to improve page load speeds.

19.6. Post Excerpts

Excerpts are short summaries of your post. Think of them in the same way as you think of a Meta Description. It should be something short and enticing to the visitor. You can add excerpts in the edit post screen. If you don't see this section, check the Screen Options.

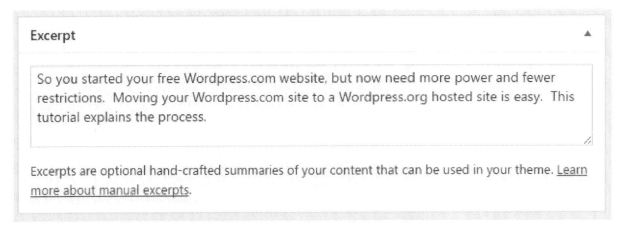

Remember, these extracts will be displayed on various areas of your website serving as descriptions for the posts. Here is the excerpt being used on my site in a recent posts list:

 <u>Moving a Site from WordPress.com to WordPress.Org</u> - So you started your free Wordpress.com website, but now need more power and fewer restrictions. Moving your Wordpress.com site to a Wordpress.org hosted site is easy. This tutorial explains the process.

Excerpts have to main purposes:

1. To add a description to the posts in your RSS feeds.

2. To supply summaries to posts in various areas of your site, like search results, tag & category pages, author pages, meta description, lists, etc.

NOTE: Using the Yoast SEO plugin, you can make Wordpress use the excerpt as a meta description.

A good reason to use excerpts is that they provide complete descriptions for any post. If you don't have excerpts written for a post, then WordPress will create a description based on the content of your page, and that will usually stop mid-word or mid-sentence.

I, therefore, recommend writing an excerpt for *all* posts on your site.

19.7. Allow Comments & Trackbacks on Posts?

You can enable or disable comments and trackbacks on posts if you want to, either globally or on a post-by-post basis. I recommend you keep comments enabled on all posts because social interaction is an important aspect of our SEO efforts.

Trackbacks are a little more difficult to give a hard and fast rule about. Essentially, a trackback is like a comment sent to your site from another site, when that other site links to yours. While it is nice to know who is linking to us, this feature has been heavily abused by spammers. This means that 99% of the time, a trackback is bogus and no link exists. The reason the spammers do this is to try to get you to approve their 'trackback', which then goes live on your site with a link back to theirs. I tend to turn trackbacks off on all posts by default because spammers were taking up too much of my time; constantly checking to see if a site had really linked to mine or not. Don't forget, you can choose whether to enable or disable globally or on a post-by-post basis.

19.8. Scheduling Posts

There may be times when you want to schedule posts into the future. For example, if I am adding 10-20 posts to my site (let's say I just got a bunch of content from my ghost writer), I would schedule those posts to be released over 2-3 weeks. Doing this encourages the search engine spiders to come back more regularly. It can also encourage visitors to return more often when they see that fresh content is being added frequently.

To schedule posts, look to the 'Publish' section located on the right of the post edit screen:

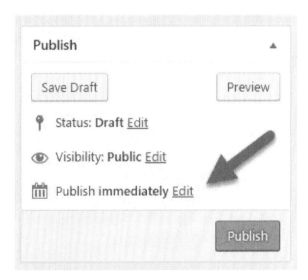

Where it says '**Publish immediately**', there is an '**Edit**' link that allows you to change the date and time of publication. The edit link expands the area:

Now you can select a date, and even a time, for when the article will be published. When that date and time arrives, WordPress automatically publishes the article for you. You do not have to login or do anything else once this is set up.

If you want to bulk schedule posts for a site, consider using the Editorial Calendar plugin.

This gives you a drag and drop calendar interface for scheduling your posts.

19.9. A Checklist for Good SEO Content

Writing good SEO content is a huge topic. In fact, I've written an entire book and video course on the subject. However, I wanted to include a quick summary of the main points you should check off as you publish content on your site.

19.9.1. Titles

☐ Titles are one of the most important areas of a web page, both in terms of SEO and getting click-throughs from the search engines. The title needs to appeal to the searcher.

☐ Titles are automatically converted into URLs by Wordpress. A setting in the Yoast SEO plugin can automatically strip out stop words from the URL. I recommend you use that (see later). Also, consider manually editing the filename to include a different keyword than the title.

☐ Include your primary keywords in the title if you can, but don't stuff it. Words that appear at the beginning of the title are given more emphasis by Google, so insert the most important keyword as close to the start of the title as possible.

- ☐ Try to minimize the use of stop words. These are the short, unimportant words that can dilute the importance of keywords. Examples include "the", "it", "of" etc.

- ☐ Limit the title to less than 60 characters in length. A good length to shoot for is 55. Any longer and it will become truncated in the search results. You can use the snippet preview supplied by the Yoast SEO plugin to help check titles.

19.9.2. Headings

- ☐ You can use H1, H2, H3, H4, H5 & H6 headings on a web page.

- ☐ Your web page should contain only one H1 heading. Most Wordpress themes automatically use if for the post title, so don't use any more H1 headings in your content.

- ☐ Use H2 and H3 in a hierarchical manner. Split up the article into sections using H2 headers. If a section needs to be further divided into sections, use H3 headers within the H2. I don't recommend you use H4, H5 or H6 headers. Wordpress themes often use these in the sidebars, and they are given very little attention by the search engines.

19.9.3. Theme Your Content

This is a huge topic! Please see my other books and courses if you want in-depth help with this. The basics are simple, though.

When you write content, don't focus on one or two keywords. Choose a topic to write about. The topic can be a broad, top-level keyword. Then find out what keywords and phrase SHOULD be included in that topic and try to incorporate as many as possible in your web page.

For example, if I had a health site, I might target the keyword "gestational diabetes". Rather than try to create a page around the term "gestational diabetes", I would find out what other words and phrases are needed to create a compressive, authoritative piece of content. They would include words like:

Blood sugar, blood pressure, hypertension, glucose, pregnancy, baby, birth, pre-eclampsia, insulin, glucose tolerance test, type 2 diabetes, screening, treatment, etc.

When writing the content, your focus should be on all of these words and phrases, not just "gestational diabetes".

19.9.4. Categories & Tags

☐ Only ever assign one category to a post. If you think your post can fit into two or more, chances are you have chosen the wrong categories.

☐ Use tags sparingly. Remember that Wordpress creates a tag page for each one used.

☐ Only ever assign a tag to a post if that tag is used (or will be used) for several posts. I would recommend 3 or 4 tags maximum per post, but you can also decide not to use tags if you prefer.

☐ Use tags to create related groups within your categories. Categories and tags should work together and complement each other.
For example, I might have a category called "Type 2 Diabetes" and tags for "symptoms", "treatment", etc.

19.9.5. Images

☐ ALT tags help the visually impaired visitors to your website. Create good, accurate ALT tags for your images. Do not try to stuff keywords into these tags.

☐ Give images a descriptive name that might contain a keyword phrase.

☐ Remember that images used in your content may be used if people share your content on social media channels.

☐ Try to include an image near the beginning of your web page. Visitors are more likely to see the image and continue reading your content than if they just see a wall of text.

☐ Optimize your images before you upload them. If your web page content loads inside an 800 pixel wide "text box" and you want the image to take up half of the width, resize the image to 400 pixels wide before uploading.

☐ If you have an image compression plugin like Smush, use it.

☐ Run your pages through GTMetrix.com to check if any images are causing page loading delays.

19.9.6. Excerpts

☐ Always include a descriptive excerpt with your posts. These can be used for post descriptions on your site, but also the meta description of the web page. Google may also use it as the description of your post in the search results.

☐ The except should be unique from the title and complement it.

☐ Imagine your excerpt appearing as your post description in Google. Try to create excerpts that entice the click from searchers.

19.9.7. Linking to Other Content

☐ The internet was built on links. Don't' be afraid to link out to web pages on authority websites using dofollow links.

☐ If you link to a page that you don't "trust", use the nofollow tag.

☐ Link to your "legal pages" using nofollow.

☐ Link to other pages on your site where appropriate. Check out how Wikipedia links to related content on Wikipedia from every page on their site. I don't recommend you internally link as much as Wikipedia, but certainly, if you have relevant content to refer to in an article, link to it. This type of internal link is the only acceptable way to get keyword rich anchor text into a link to your own content. The C.I. Backlinks plugin mentioned on the resources page for this book is a great way of automating this in a natural way.

☐ Use YARPP or a similar plugin to provide relevant links to related content.

20. Setting up Category Pages

Categories are used to classify posts. When you create a new post, you file it away in a particular category. As your site grows, categories will start to fill up with more and more relevant, related content.

For every category you create, WordPress will create a 'category page'. This will list all of the posts within that category.

This helps visitors and search engines alike.

When you set up a category on your site, I highly recommend you give your new category a description.

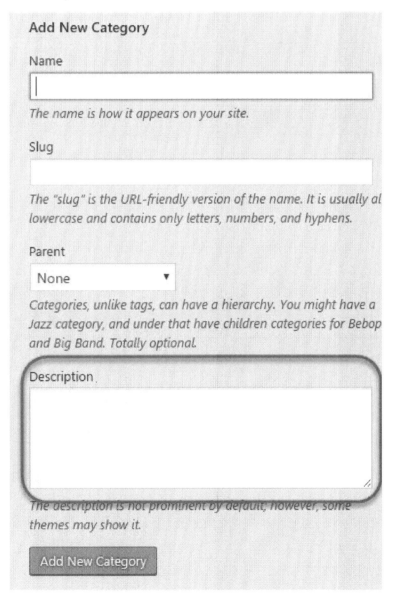

Some themes will use these descriptions in a variety of place, but the most important place is the category page itself, as an introduction. If your theme supports this, and I suggest you find one that does, your category pages suddenly become a lot more useful and interesting to visitors and search engines.

That is, as long as it doesn't force full post content on you.

20.1. A Category Page Full Post Content

A typical category page looks something like this, with or without the introduction at the top:

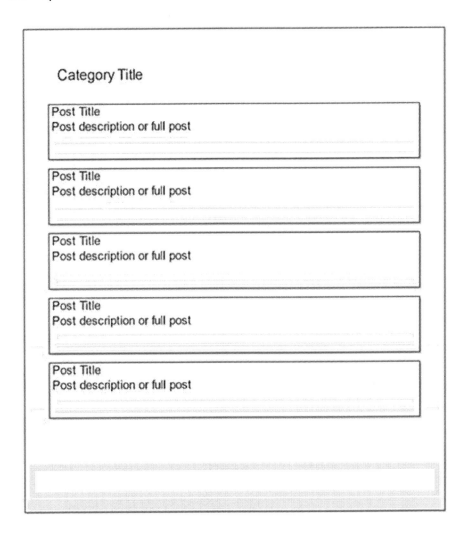

Depending on the theme you are using, those posts may be showing as a title with an excerpt, or a title with a full post. Obviously, the latter would cause huge duplication problems since these category pages would contain the complete text of all posts within the category.

You should choose a theme that allows you to use post excerpts on category (and tag) pages. If you don't have a choice and the theme displays full posts on these pages, then these pages won't serve as useful content. Instead, they'll cause you a nightmare of duplication problems that Google will not be happy about.

There is a solution, though.

If your category page uses the full post text, then you should set the category pages (and probably tag pages) to noindex, *follow*. This means that search engines will find them and follow the links on these pages, but won't index and include them in the search results. Since we only want valuable pages/posts to appear in the search engine, this is what we want.

Thanks to the Yoast SEO plugin, achieving this is easy.

The Yoast SEO plugin allows you to treat categories and tag pages globally, or on a one-by-one basis. Therefore, you can globally set all category pages to *noindex, follow*, or you can set just one or two category pages to *noindex, follow*. The same goes for tag pages, posts, pages, etc.

20.1.1. Globally Set All Category Pages to Noindex, Follow

To make *all* category page *noindex, follow*, go to the **SEO -> Titles & Metas** section, and click on the '**Taxonomies**' tab.

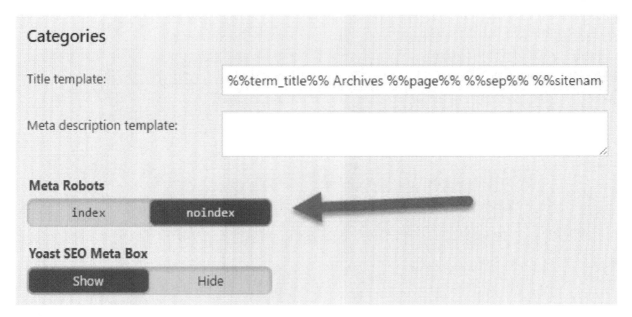

Set the **Meta Robots** option to "noindex".

If you need to do this to tag pages as well, set the **Meta Robots** on the Tags to "noindex" as well.

Now, all category pages (and tag pages) will have code included in the web page to stop search engine spiders indexing the content. That means they won't appear in the search engines.

Although probably less useful for most websites, you can also set category and tab pages to noindex on a one-by-one basis.

20.1.2. Setting Individual Category Pages to Noindex, Follow

To make category pages *noindex, follow* on a one-by-one basis, you need to go to the **Posts -> Categories** section of the Dashboard, and click on a category's '**Edit**' link for the one you want to modify.

Note: You need to create the category first, and then go in and edit it, because these extra options are not found on the main screen from where you create new categories.

When you go into the category edit screen, there are a number of new options available to you thanks to Yoast's SEO plugin. These should look very familiar to you:

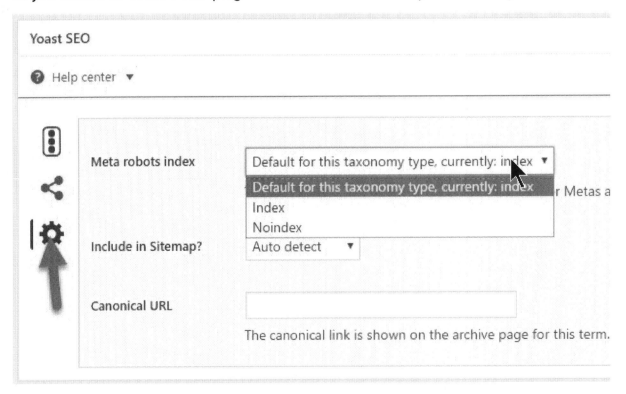

The options in this Yoast SEO box allow us to override any or all of the global category settings. On a one-by-one basis, we can define a custom Title and Description (using the snippet editor), set the Facebook title, description and image, make the category page *noindex*, and exclude it from the sitemap. These are the exact same settings you have for every post and page on your site too!

NOTE: If you *noindex, follow,* your category pages, I don't recommend excluding the category pages from the sitemap. Google will find the category pages in the sitemap and then spider them to find all of your content. But Google won't index and rank these pages, which is what we want.

20.2. The Ideal Category Page?

A category page becomes useful when it includes:

☐ An Introduction

☐ A list of posts in the category, with hyperlinked title to the article and a short description (excerpt).

Our category pages would then look like this:

In this category page, there is a text introduction to the category, followed by post Titles and post Excerpts of all the articles within the category.

The written introduction adds SEO benefits, in that this page now has some unique content on it, and introduces the posts in the category to both visitors and search engines. This is the type of category (and tag) page that I strive for on all of my own websites. Set up this way, you can leave *all* of the category pages as *index, follow*. This is because they are now genuinely useful pages for a visitor.

To get this type of category page, your theme needs to:

☐ Give you the option of using excerpts (instead of full posts), on category and tag pages.

☐ Include the category introduction at the top of the category page.

I cannot stress enough how important I think it is to have a theme that meets these two simple criteria. Category and tag pages can rank really well, so are a valuable asset to your site to attract website visitors.

Assuming your theme meets these criteria, your category page should look something like this:

Probiotics

Probiotics are the good bacteria in your gut that represent your first line of defenses against disease, and a whole host of other health benefits.

When most people think of probiotics, they think of yoghurt drinks, and manufactured products often containing lactobacilli. Did you know that the lactobacilli were grown and harvested in a lab, and then added to the drink (the drink is a good medium to support the life of the bacteria)?

Another thing to think about is how good bacteria got into our gut in the first place. Over the centuries, bacteria on the food we ate (before we became germophobic) would colonise and populate our gut, providing huge benefits. Doesn't it make more sense then to re-populate our gut bacteria with bacteria that originate in the soil? Well, with our soils widely depleted of good bacteria through over-zealous, profit-inducing use of herbicides and pesticides, this is not as easy as you might think.

The following articles are about probiotics and you can read more about prebiotics here, if interested. If you have any comments or questions, please leave a comment at the end of the relevant article and I'll do my best to answer it.

Probiotics for Acne – Do they Work?

Quite a high percentage of acne sufferers are victims of poor gut health. Studies show that probiotics can help to treat these skin conditions.

Probiotics for Treating Bloating Bellies

Bloating can be the result of an imbalance in your gut flora. Studies show that probiotics bifidobacterium infantis are effective at treating the condition.

Probiotics for the Treatment of Constipation

Trails which study probiotics for constipation have shown promise in some cases. Is this the all-natural remedy sufferers have been looking for?

Notice the introduction at the top of the category page, followed by links to the posts in that category, with a short excerpt being used as the description.

20.3. Formatting the introduction

When you create a category, the description box is a plain text editor, meaning you cannot really format your descriptions. You can try to add in some HTML if you know how to code in HTML, but it is unreliable, and much of it will be stripped out. To illustrate this, here is a simple description that I've tried to format with HTML.

```
<p>Nunc congue turpis quis nulla rutrum auctor. <a href="http://lorem.com">Sed mattis</a>
malesuada nunc. Nulla pretium dapibus nibh ut commodo.  </p>

<h2>Phasellus et consequat ipsum</h2>
<p>Sed quis turpis nec velit sagittis suscipit. Cum sociis natoque penatibus et magnis dis parturient
montes, nascetur ridiculus mus.</p>
```

You can see that in the first paragraph, I've included a hyperlink. There is also an H2 header, followed by another paragraph.

If I save that and load the category page, this is how it appears:

CATEGORY: CENTERS

Nunc congue turpis quis nulla rutrum auctor. Sed mattis malesuada nunc. Nulla pretium dapibus nibh ut commodo.

Phasellus et consequat ipsum
Sed quis turpis nec velit sagittis suscipit. Cum sociis natoque penatibus et magnis dis parturient montes, nascetur ridiculus mus.

The hyperlink worked, but the H2 header didn't.

There is a way, though, and it is already installed in your Dashboard. It's the Yoast SEO plugin to the rescue again.

Go back to the **Posts** -> **Categories** screen, and click on the category you want to edit.

Thanks to the Yoast SEO plugin (make sure it is installed and activated), you know have a WYSIWYG editor for your descriptions:

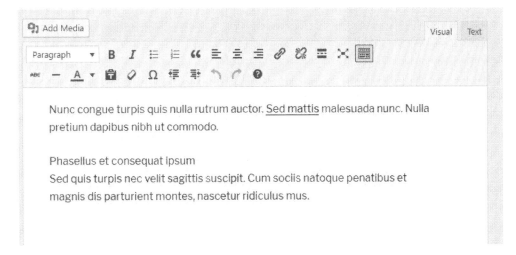

To access this WYSIWYG editor for descriptions (and tag pages), you need to create the category first, then go in and edit it.

Using this editor, I can format it the way I previously wanted to:

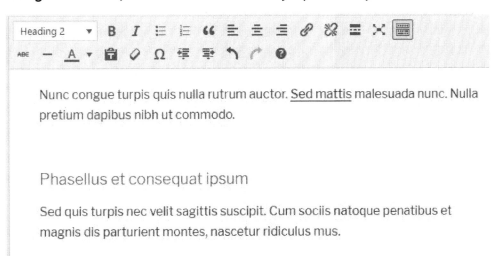

If I visit the category page now, you can see the formatting remains:

CATEGORY: CENTERS

Nunc congue turpis quis nulla rutrum auctor. Sed mattis malesuada nunc. Nulla pretium dapibus nibh ut commodo.

Phasellus et consequat ipsum

Sed quis turpis nec velit sagittis suscipit. Cum sociis natoque penatibus et magnis dis parturient montes, nascetur ridiculus mus.

The editor will also allow you to insert images and any other formatting that you normally have available to you when entering posts or pages.

Using this powerful category (and tag) page description editor, it's possible to create great, interesting, and valuable introductions for all category and tags pages.

21. Tag Pages

We've just seen how to create valuable category pages that can (and deserve to) rank well in the search engines. Tag pages can rank remarkably well because they tend to have a lot of internal links pointing at them (from all posts that use that tag). With the added introduction, they become really valuable pages. For this reason, I like to have tag pages set up in the exact same way we did for category pages.

The process is identical to category pages.

If you go and edit an existing tag (**Posts -> Tags**), you'll get the same Yoast SEO settings we saw with the category pages, allowing you to create a custom Title and Description as well as being able to *noindex* a tag page and exclude it from the sitemap if you need to.

To be useful, the theme's tag page needs to meet the same two criteria:

☐ Give you the option of using excerpts (instead of full posts), on tag pages.

☐ Include the tag introduction at the top of the tag page.

Just follow the same advice for tags as we discussed for category pages. If tag pages meet these criteria, use them. If not, noindex them.

22. WordPress SEO Plugin Setup

Yoast's SEO plugin provides a massive amount of SEO control over your WordPress site. When you install it, you'll find SEO options popping up in several areas of your Dashboard (as we've already seen). These areas can be divided into two main parts; those that control settings globally, and those that control settings on a one-by-one basis.

We've already seen how the plugin can be used to change the SEO settings on a post-by-post, page-by-page or archive-by-archive (category & tag pages), so let's focus now on the global settings.

22.1. Dashboard Settings

The 'Global' settings are found in the SEO menu of the WP Dashboard:

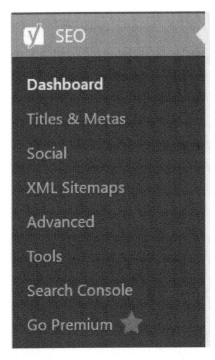

When you first install and activate the plugin, you may only see this:

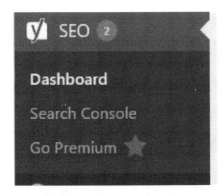

That's because, for some strange reason, the plugin turns off most of the useful features by default. It's easy enough to fix.

Click on **Dashboard** and select the **Features** tab across the top:

On this page, there are three options. The top option (Advanced settings pages) is the one that is responsible for hiding most of the plugin options.

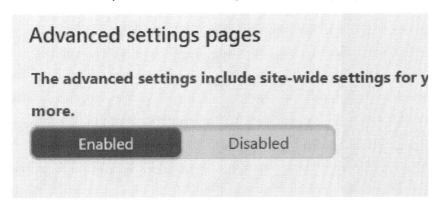

Enable it and save the options. All of the SEO menu items will appear.

I recommend you enable all three options on this page.

OK, with all of the SEO plugin options now visible, let's look at them all.

Be aware that any changes you make inside these "global" settings, will apply across your whole site.

Changes making the category pages noindex will mean ALL category pages on the site will be noindex. However, we can override global settings on a category-by-category basis, as shown earlier in the book.

For category and tag pages, you can override global settings by going in and editing the category or tag, after its initial creation. We saw this earlier.

For posts and pages, you'll find the global override settings on the '**Edit Post**' and '**Edit Page**' screens. Those settings look like this:

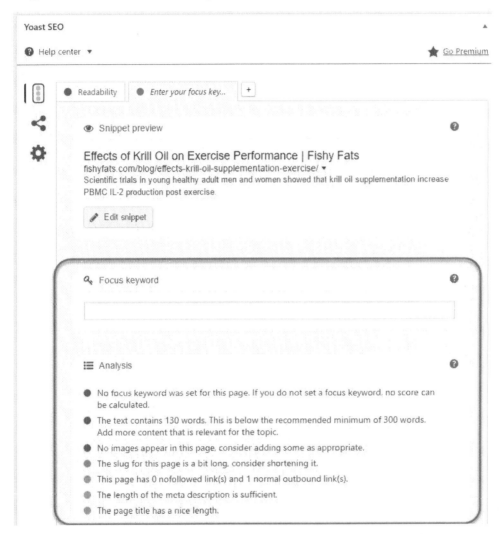

The options are on three tabs in the top left position – we've seen that already.

In my screenshot, there is a "focus" keyword section at the bottom. That is something you may or may not have, depending on your settings within the SEO plugin. I personally will turn this off (I'll show you how later), as I don't optimize content for specific keywords. That's the old way of doing SEO, and can be dangerous if you don't know what you are doing (or basing your SEO on advice from a plugin).

Changes made in these settings will only affect the page or post you are editing. In other words, these settings will override the global settings for this post or page.

OK, let's look at the 'Global Settings'.

Click on **SEO -> Dashboard**. Across the top, you'll see several tabs that give you access to various settings. You are currently on the Dashboard tab. This is used to notify you of problems, or other notifications. For example, in the **Notifications** section, you can see one that offers to help you configure the plugin:

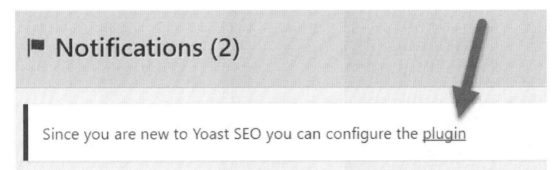

We are going to go through the configuration wizard so you can see what it covers. This is not essential as we will go through all of the settings manually. Therefore, you can skip this if you want.

If you want to go through the wizard, be aware that it will try to connect the SEO plugin to your Google Search Console account, so make sure you have your site added and authenticated inside GSC before running the wizard.

OK, let's start. Click on the "plugin" link to start the configuration wizard.

Step 1 will ask you to sign up for their newsletter. If you want to sign up, do. If you don't want to, click **Next**. You'll be taken to the "environment" screen:

Environment

Please specify the environment in which this site - http://█████████ - is running.

- ⦿ Production (this is a live site with real traffic)
- ○ Staging (this is a copy of a live site used for testing purposes only)
- ○ Development (this site is running locally for development purposes)

Select the option that applies (probably "production"), and click **Next**. You'll be asked what type of site you are setting up:

Site type

What kind of site is http://▮▮▮▮▮▮▮?

○ Blog
○ Webshop
○ News site
◉ Small business site
○ Other corporate site
○ Other personal site

Select the most appropriate option, and click **next**.

Note that you can change these settings later, so don't worry too much if you are unsure of any settings.

The next screen is asking whether you are a company or a person:

Company or person

This data is shown as metadata in your site. It is intended to appear in Google's Knowledge Graph. You can be either a company, or a person, choose either:

○ Company
◉ Person

The name of the person

[   ]

It will ask you for the name of the company or person. If you chose company, it will also ask if you want to upload a company logo. Click **Next** when you have filled in the form. You'll be taken to the social profiles section:

Social profiles

Please add all your relevant social profiles. We use these to let search engines know about them, and to enhance your social metadata:

Facebook Page URL

[   ]

Twitter Username

[   ]

Instagram URL

[   ]

I've only shown a small part of that screen. There are a lot more options. This screen asks you for the URLs of your social channels. These include Facebook page, Twitter, Instagram, LinkedIn, MySpace, Pinterest, Youtube, and Google+.

Enter any that you have. You can always go in manually later and add these too. Click **Next** when you are finished. You'll now be taken to the post type visibility settings:

Post type visibility

Please specify which of the following public post types you would like Google to see.

The post type "Posts" should be

- ⊙ Visible
- ○ Hidden

The post type "Pages" should be

- ⊙ Visible
- ○ Hidden

The post type "Media" should be

- ○ Visible
- ⊙ Hidden

WordPress automatically generates an URL for each media item in the library. Enabling this will allow for google to index the generated URL.

PREVIOUS   NEXT

I recommend you leave these as they are for now. We will go in manually later and consider changing the "pages" visibility, but I want to discuss that with you before making the change. Click **Next** when ready and you'll be taken to the "multiple authors" screen:

Multiple authors

Does, or will, your site have multiple authors?

- ○ Yes
- ⊙ No

Make your selection and click **Next**. You'll be taken to the Google Search Console screen. This allows the plugin to see your search console information. Note that you need to have your website already set up and authenticated in your GSC account:

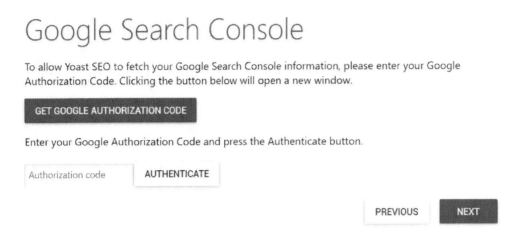

Click the **Get Google Authorization Code** and a window opens up, asking you to login to your search console. Once logged in, you'll then be asked for permission:

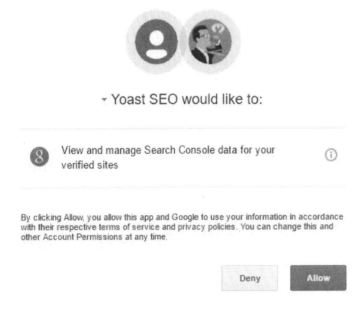

Click the **Allow** button to proceed.

You'll be given an authentication code. Paste it into the form in the SEO plugin settings, and click **Authenticate**.

Enter your Google Authorization Code and press

AUTHENTICATE

You will then be asked to choose which profile represents the site you are setting up:

Google Search Console

Select profile

Choose a profile ▼

REAUTHENTICATE WITH GOOGLE

Select your profile from your GSC account. If you do not see the site listed, then you haven't set it up in your GSC account. You can just click **Next** to skip this step if you don't want to do that now.

On the next screen, you'll be asked to choose a title separator character:

Title settings

Website name

My site

Title Separator

| - | – | — | · | • | * | ★ | \| | ~ | « | » | < | > |

Choose the symbol to use as your title separator. This will display, for instance, between your post title and site name. Symbols are shown in the size they'll appear in the search results.

When someone visits your website, Wordpress creates the page on-the-fly. It builds the title of the page according to the settings you have in the SEO plugin. By default, the title may include the post title and site name. What you are choosing in these settings is the character that would appear between post title and site name in the title. Make your choice and click **Next**.

That completes the wizard. Scroll to the bottom of the "Success" page, and click the link to "Go back to the Yoast SEO dashboard".

We are now back where we started in the Dashboard settings. Some of the settings in the plugin will have been updated, depending on your choices, but we can go in and manually change anything.

Let's work out way through the settings.

Click the **General** tab across the top:

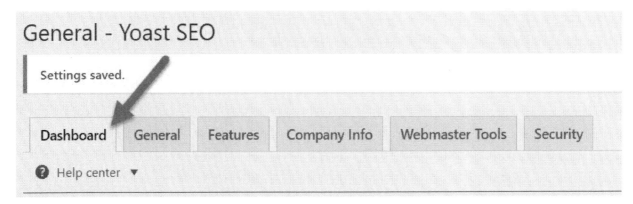

NOTE: There is a help center link in that screenshot. Clicking that link will provide context-sensitive help, which is great if you get stuck.

On the **General** tab, you can re-run the configuration wizard if you want to. You can also reset the plugin settings to their defaults.

Click on the **Features** tab. There are three settings on this screen.

Advanced settings pages – hides/unhides some of the more useful settings of the plugin. This should be enabled.

Onpage.org – This is a service that can check your site is online and available. You can enable this if you want.

Admin bar menu – The admin bar is a really useful bar that appears across the top of your site when you are logged in. It's great when you are browsing your website. It looks like this:

With the menu bar visible, you can quickly add/edit posts/pages as you browse your site, clear the cache (if you are using W3 Total Cache which we'll set up in the next chapter) and get quick access to important areas of your Wordpress Dashboard. Make sure this one is enabled.

Click on the **Company Info** tab.

If you went through the wizard, you will see your information is already in this form. You can edit that information here.

This screen allows you to change the name of your site, company, company logo, or personal name.

Click on the **Webmaster Tools** tab.

This screen allows you to verify your site with various webmaster tools. If you went through the wizard, you may already have verified with Google Search Console. This screen also allows you to verify with Bing Webmaster Tools and Yandex Webmaster Tools if you use them.

Click on the **Security** tab.

This tab has one setting. If you have multiple authors on your site, and you don't 100% trust them, then disable this option. That will prevent anyone but yourself from changing the indexable status of posts.

OK, we've finished going through the Dashboard settings of the SEO plugin. Let's move to the next set of settings.

Click on **Titles & Metas** in the sidebar menu.

22.2. Title & Metas

The 'Titles' and 'Metas' section has a lot of options, spread over several tabs.

On the General tab, you can see the title separator option at the top. We saw this option in the configuration wizard, but you can manually change it here if you want.

Underneath you'll find two other settings in the "Enabled analysis" section.

Readability analysis checks your content and makes suggestions. You'll find these suggestions on the edit post screen, inside the Yoast SEO box. Here is the readability analysis for one of my articles:

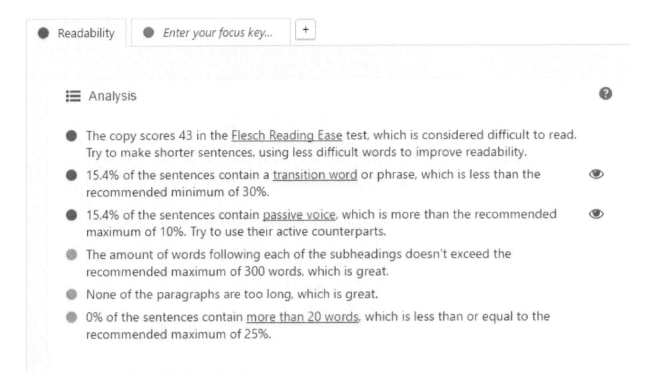

If this is useful to you, keep that option checked in the SEO plugin settings.

The keyword analysis option, in my view, is a little dangerous. It gets you focusing on specific keywords. In the previous screenshot, you can see there is a tab at the top to enter a focus keyword. The idea is that the plugin will tell you how well your content is optimized for that keyword. Here is an analysis for my web page:

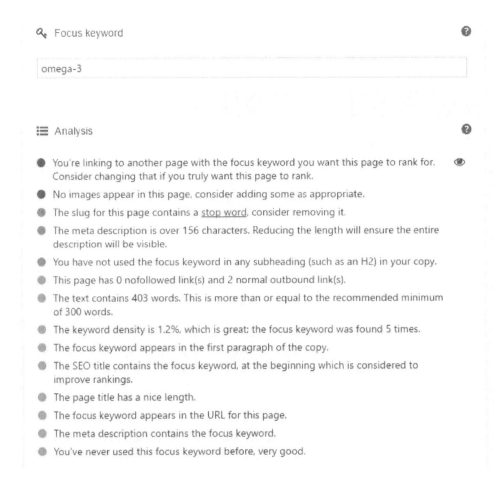

Some of that information is useful, like the fact my meta description is a little long. However, advice on article length, keyword density, and positioning of the keyword in the elements on the page are dangerous.

Focusing on a single keyword when optimizing a web page is dangerous and could get your site penalized. Check out my writing web content book or course if you want to learn how I do this.

If you've made any changes to the General tab, save them. Then click on the **Homepage** tab.

If you are using your recent posts as the homepage, you will see this:

Homepage

Title template: %%sitename%% %%page%% %%sep%% %%sitedesc%%

Meta description template:

Save Changes

This allows you to set a template for the title and description of your homepage.

You can see some variable being used. If you click on the help link, you can find a full list of basic and advanced variables for use in your templates.

Essentially these variable as swapped out for the specific piece of data when the page is rendered in a web browser. For example, %%sitename%% will be replaced with the actual site name, %%sep%% will be replaced with the separator character you chose. But you don't have to use variables.

We could define the title template as:

%%sitename%% :: Making your dog happier

If your site name was '**Doggy Treats**', then when the homepage was loaded in a browser, the homepage title would display as:

Doggy Treats :: Making your dog happier

We could, of course, use a variable to insert the tagline of the site into the title:

%%sitename%% :: %%sitesdesc%%

The title would then pull the site name and tagline from the '**General Settings**' tab of your WP Dashboard, and create the title from those.

Now, you might ask why bother using variables for the homepage title when you can just type in the *exact title* you want. The main reason is in case you ever update the site title or tagline in your settings. By using variables, our titles will automatically get updated, without us having to remember to go in and manually change them.

The plugin sets the default homepage title as follows:

%%sitename%% %%page%% %%sep%% %%sitedesc%%

By looking at the variable list on the '**Help**' tab, you can decode this to see that the homepage title would be the site name, followed by a separator, and then the site description (tagline). The **%%page%%** variable is not relevant to the homepage so it will be blank (I personally remove that variable from the homepage title template).

The default homepage title is OK and I would leave it as it is if I were you. For the description, you can use variables if you want, or just type in the description as you want it to appear on the homepage.

If you are using a static page as your homepage, you will see this:

Homepage & Front page

You can determine the title and description for the front page by editing the front page itself »

Save Changes

If you want to make changes to title or description of the homepage, go in and make them on the edit page screen.

Click on the **Post Types** tab. This is where you can define the title and description templates to posts, pages, and media items. You can also control the meta robots settings.

Since I like my websites to be 'branded' by the site's name, I always include the **%%sitename%%** variable in the title of my posts, usually at the end of the title template. The template that is used by default is actually quite good because it uses the posts title and the site name.

For the post description, I use **%%excerpt%%**. This will then use whatever excerpt I have entered for a post as the Meta Description tag.

Here is my completed posts section:

Posts

Title template:

%%title%% %%page%% %%sep%% %%sitename%%

Meta description template:

%%excerpt%%

Meta Robots

| index | noindex |

Date in Snippet Preview

| Show | Hide |

Yoast SEO Meta Box

| Show | Hide |

The **Meta Robots** should be set to **index**. That will ensure the search engines include the posts in the search results.

The **Date in Snippet Preview** is up to you. The snippet is what Google shows in the search results. If your content is time-sensitive, maybe you want this enabled. If, like me, your content is timeless ;) leave this as **hide**. We don't want searchers to be alerted to the fact that our post is 2 years old!

The **Yoast SEO Meta Box** should be left to **Show**. This means the SEO settings will be available to us on the edit post screen.

For pages, I use the same title & meta description templates as for posts.

However, the I only use pages for my legal pages. These are pages like contact, privacy, terms, etc. I don't want these being indexed in Google. I only want Google to index my money pages. Therefore, I set the **Meta Robots** to noindex.

Here are my page settings:

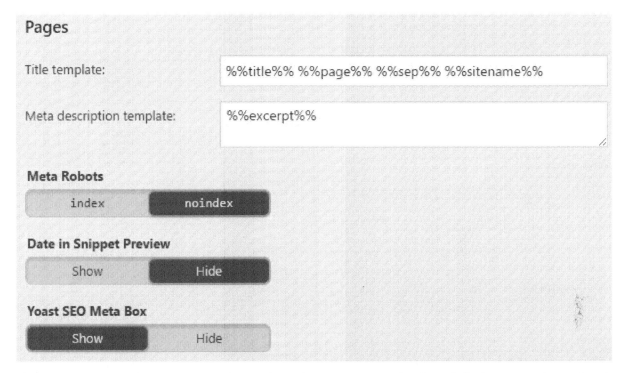

If I have a page that I want to be indexed, I can override this global setting by going in and editing the SEO settings on the edit page screen.

"Media" are special posts created by WordPress to hold information about the media you upload. I don't want mine indexed as separate pages, so here are the settings I use:

Media

Title template:
%%title%% %%page%% %%sep%% %%sitename%%

Meta description template:
%%caption%%

Meta Robots

index | noindex

Date in Snippet Preview

Show | Hide

Yoast SEO Meta Box

Show | Hide

You can see a new variable there. Guess what %%caption%% is?

We've finished with the **Post Types** settings. Let's move on to the Taxonomies.

Under the **Taxonomies** tab, we can set up the global options for Categories, Tags, and Format.

For categories, the title template is fine. I do change mine a little. Here is one that I might use:

Category :: %%term_title%% %%page%% %%sep%% %%sitename%%

Notice that the word category is not a variable.

The **%%term_title%%** variable will be replaced by the category title/name.

A typical category page title from that template might look like this:

Category :: Health Benefits | Fishy Fats

This title tells my visitors and search engines that the page is the "health benefits" category page, on the Fishy Fats website.

Here are my settings for Categories:

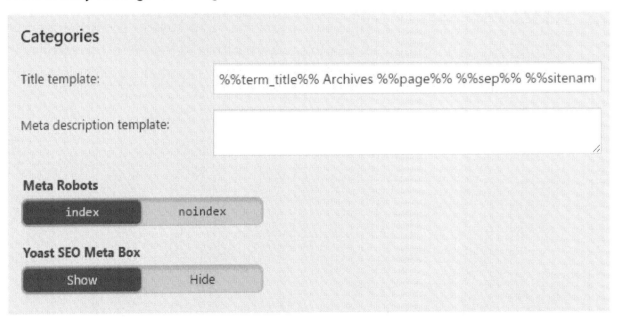

A common template for the meta description is to use the **%%category_description%%** variable. This will be replaced by the description we entered for the category. I recommend you don't do this, as we are using that description as the category page introduction. We don't want the entire introduction also included in the HTML as the meta description. For that reason, leave the meta description template empty.

IMPORTANT REMINDER: I have my category pages set globally to be indexed. That is because I set them up to include an introduction at the top, followed by post excerpts (See the category setup section of this book if you need to recap). If you do not use an introduction & post excerpts on your category pages, set the **Meta Robots** to noindex.

My tag page settings are similar to my category page settings. The only slight difference is the in the title. My tag page title template is usually something like:

Articles about %%term_title%% %%page%% %%sep%% %%sitename%%

Here are my Tags settings:

Tags

Title template:	Articles about %%term_title%% %%page%% %%sep%% %%siti
Meta description template:	

Meta Robots

index	noindex

Yoast SEO Meta Box

Show	Hide

Again, I have my tag pages set to be indexed. That is only because I have an introduction on all of my tag pages, followed by excerpts of the posts using that tag (see the tag page setup section of this book if you need to recap). If you do not have introductory text on your tag pages, set the **Meta Robots** to noindex.

The Format options under the 'Taxonomies' tab can be left unchanged.

Click on the **Archives** tab. This is where you control the settings for some special pages on your site:

☐ Author archives are pages set up for each author on a site, which lists their posts.

☐ Date archives are pages set up to list all posts made on a given date.

☐ Special pages are the search page and 404 error pages.

Here are my settings for author archives:

Note that I have set these pages to noindex, even though I have author archives enabled. That is because I don't want the author archive pages to get into the search engines, as it would only add to the duplicate content problem. However, with these setting, Google can still follow the links on the page to help with the spidering of the site.

Since I have this set as noindex, there is no need to enter a Meta Description here.

For 'Date Archives', I use these settings:

Again, this is noindex to reduce the duplicate content in Google.

The last couple of options are for the 'Special Pages'. You can leave the default settings for these two.

Make sure you click **Save Changes** if you've made any.

Now click on the **Other** tab. This page gives us a few more options. The only change I would recommend is to noindex subpages of archives. Click **Save Changes** when you've done that, and we'll move onto the **Social** options.

22.3. Social Settings

Click on the **Social** link in the SEO menu located left of the WP Dashboard. The social settings are spread over several tabs:

On the **Accounts tab**, you can connect your site to Facebook, Twitter, Google+, and other social media channels. If you went through the configuration wizard, you may already have these populated. However, this screen allows you to come in and manually update/edit/add social URLs.

Once you are done, click on the **Facebook** tab.

Facebook's Open Graph is used by a lot of search engines and social websites to tell them information about your site and about the pages they are visiting.

On the Facebook tab, check the box at the top to **Add Open Graph Data**. Note that there are a number of plugins that offer to add this data to your pages. Only enable it in one plugin (this SEO plugin).

With this checked, the plugin will add Facebook Open Graph Meta Tags to your pages:

```
https://yoast.com/wordpress/plugins/seo/ -->
<meta name="description" content="Krill Oil v Fish Oil - The Story There
so much is being written about krill oil and fish oil; both are excellen
fa"/>
<meta name="robots" content="noindex,follow,noodp"/>
<link rel="canonical" href="http://fishyfats.com/" />
<meta property="og:locale" content="en_US" />
<meta property="og:type" content="website" />
<meta property="og:title" content="Krill Oil v Fish Oil - The Story | Fi:
<meta property="og:description" content="Krill Oil v Fish Oil - The Story
reason why so much is being written about krill oil and fish oil; both a
Omega-3 fa" />
<meta property="og:url" content="http://fishyfats.com/" />
<meta property="og:site_name" content="Fishy Fats" />
<meta property="og:image" content="http://fishyfats.com/wp-content/uploa
3.jpg" />
<meta name="twitter:card" content="summary" />
<meta name="twitter:description" content="Krill Oil v Fish Oil - The Stor
reason why so much is being written about krill oil and fish oil; both a
Omega-3 fa" />
```

Under the Open Graph settings, you can upload a default image. This will be used when someone shares content on your site to Facebook, but the post doesn't have any of its own images that can be used. I highly recommend you upload a default image.

What you do next depends on how you have your Facebook set up. Personally, I have a Facebook 'page' for each of my websites, and I recommend you do the same. You can then '**Add a Facebook Admin**' by clicking the button, and following the instructions on the screen. Once you have connected your site to your Facebook profile, you can then add the Facebook Page URL in the settings. This will link the content on your site to your Facebook page and more meta data will be added to your page.

OK, that's all we are doing on the Facebook tab. Let's move over to the Twitter tab.

You can leave these settings on the default. This will add Twitter meta data to your web pages.

```
<meta name="twitter:card" content="summary" />
<meta name="twitter:description" content="Omega-3 fatty acids
required by every cell in your body. This article discusses wt
3." />
<meta name="twitter:title" content="Omega-3 deficiency | Fish)
<meta name="twitter:site" content="@FishyFats" />
<meta name="twitter:image" content="http://fishyfats.com/wp-cc
<meta name="twitter:creator" content="@FishyFats" />
<!-- / Yoast SEO plugin. -->
```

When anyone tweets with a link to your site, the tweet will contain the usual stuff, but Twitter also scrapes the card data. When viewing the Tweet, the default view is the summary of the tweet (140 characters), but that can now be expanded to show the full Twitter card data.

For more information on Twitter cards, I suggest you read this post on the Twitter website:

https://dev.twitter.com/docs/cards

The next tab is the **Pinterest** options.

This screen lets you confirm your site with Pinterest. Just follow the instruction on this page.

Finally, we have the Google + settings.

If you have set up a business page on Google Plus for your website, add the URL of the page here. You should also provide a link to your site from your Google+ about page.

22.4. XML Sitemap Settings

From the SEO menu on the left of the WP Dashboard, select **XML Sitemaps**. Again, these settings are spread across multiple tabs:

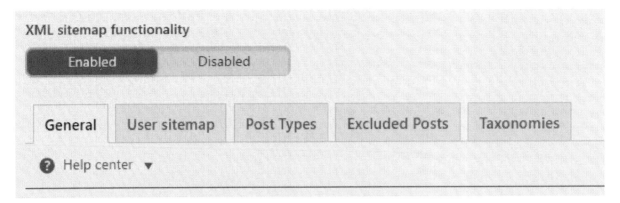

First things first, at the very top, make sure the XML sitemap functionality is enabled.

Having an XML sitemap for your site is really important. While it's not much use to visitors, it's a big help to search engines, as they use it to find your site's content.

With good navigation on your site, a search box, and a well-designed homepage, your visitors should not need a sitemap in order to find your content!

The settings on the **General** tab can be left at the default values.

Click on the **User sitemap** tab.

This has one option. I recommend you disable author/user sitemap. It's not needed as all links will be found in the main posts sitemap generated by this plugin.

On the **Post Types** tab, we have three options. Here is how I set them up:

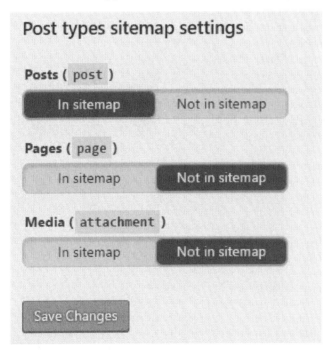

I have pages excluded from my sitemap because they are not important. All of my visitor-focused stuff is in posts. If you use pages differently, you will want to include them in the sitemap. However, remember that all global settings can be overridden. If there are one or two pages you want in the sitemap, you can set this on the edit page screen inside the Yoast SEO settings:

On the **Excluded Posts** tab, you can specify specific posts or pages to exclude from the sitemap. Just enter in the post ID (a number) in the box. Separate post IDs with a comma if you have several. You can find the post ID by visiting the **Posts -> All Posts** screen and moving your mouse over the post titles. The Post ID is shown in the bottom left of your browser window:

In the above example, the Post ID is 226. It's the number after the **post=** bit of the URL.

On the **Taxonomies** tab, you can define whether sitemaps are created for categories, tags, and format. You can leave these at their default values.

When you have finished, click the '**Save Settings**' button.

You can grab the URL of your sitemap and submit them to Google. You can find the sitemap on the general tab of the **XML Sitemaps** screen:

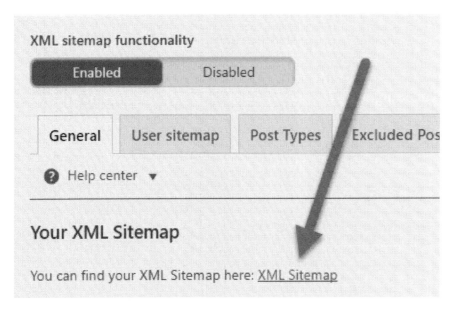

This opens the sitemap in your default web browser.

XML Sitemap

Generated by **YoastSEO**, this is an XML Sitemap, meant for consumption by search engines.

You can find more information about XML sitemaps on **sitemaps.org**.

This XML Sitemap Index file contains 3 sitemaps.

Sitemap	Last Modified
http://fishyfats.com/post-sitemap.xml	2017-01-18 11:18 +00:00
http://fishyfats.com/category-sitemap.xml	2017-01-18 11:18 +00:00
http://fishyfats.com/post_tag-sitemap.xml	2016-10-14 10:19 +00:00

You can see three sitemaps listed in that screenshot. Yoast SEO creates separate sitemaps for posts, pages, categories, tags, etc. In that list, each of those is a separate sitemap and you can click the link to see what is contained in each sitemap. For example, my tag sitemap looks like this:

XML Sitemap

Generated by **YoastSEO**, this is an XML Sitemap, meant for consumption by sear

You can find more information about XML sitemaps on **sitemaps.org**.

This XML Sitemap contains 2 URLs.

↑ **Sitemap Index**

URL
http://fishyfats.com/tag/cholesterol/
http://fishyfats.com/tag/scientific-literature/

On this particular site, I've only used 2 tags!

22.4.1. Submitting Your Sitemap(s) to Google

Earlier in the book, I recommended you sign up for Google Search Console (GSC). One of the reasons was to submit your sitemap(s) to Google so that your site would be spidered and indexed quicker. By submitting your sitemap to Google, you are telling them directly that these are the important URLs for them to consider.

The first step is to login to GSC and select the site you are working on. Then, in the side menu, go to **Crawl -> Sitemaps**.

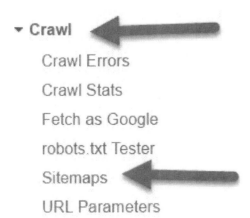

In the top right of the sitemaps screen, you'll see a button to **Add/Test Sitemap**. Click it now.

Complete the URL of your sitemap, and then click on the **Submit** button.

NOTE: If you prefer, you can click the **Test** button first to make sure you are using the correct URL, and that Google can crawl the sitemap properly. If you do that, just repeat the steps above to submit it once you are sure your sitemap status is okay.

Your newly submitted sitemap will be shown as pending. It usually takes a minute or two for Google to visit the sitemap and report back, so just wait a couple of minutes, and then refresh your browser. You should then see confirmation that Google processed your sitemap. As Google spiders your site, this table will populate to give you more details:

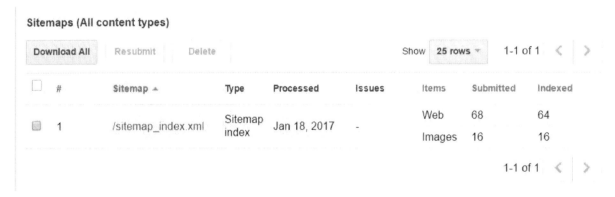

NOTE: If you have the '**Google XML Sitemap for Videos**' plugin installed, you can also submit your video sitemap in the same way.

22.5. Advanced Settings

Click on the **Advanced** menu in the sidebar. These settings are spread across three tabs:

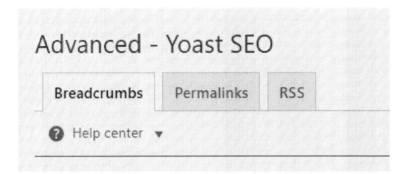

Advanced - Yoast SEO

| Breadcrumbs | Permalinks | RSS |

? Help center ▼

On the **Breadcrumb** tab, you can use the SEO plugin to insert breadcrumbs navigation in your web pages. This is beyond the scope of the book so I recommend you check out the instructions provided if you want to do this. Most themes come with breadcrumb navigation anyway, so chances are you won't need to manually insert them.

On the **Permalinks** tab, you have a few options. Permalinks are the URLs of your web pages.

Remember when we set up the permalinks, I told you that category page URLs included the word 'category' in them? We had the opportunity to change that word to anything we chose, by entering a 'category base word'. Yoast's plugin also allows you to remove the word 'category' altogether from all the category pages.

This is the first option on the **Permalinks** settings screen.

Personally, I think the word 'category' helps both the search engines and site visitors, to know exactly where they are. Therefore, these are the settings I recommend:

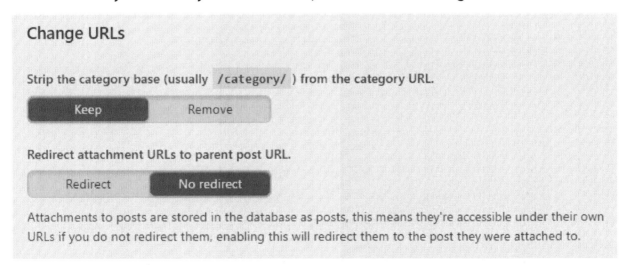

Change URLs

Strip the category base (usually `/category/`) from the category URL.

[Keep | Remove]

Redirect attachment URLs to parent post URL.

[Redirect | No redirect]

Attachments to posts are stored in the database as posts, this means they're accessible under their own URLs if you do not redirect them, enabling this will redirect them to the post they were attached to.

The next options offer to clean up the permalinks. For example, you can get the plugin to automatically strip out stop words (small insignificant words) from the URLs as they are created. This is a good idea. Therefore, these are my recommended settings for permalinks:

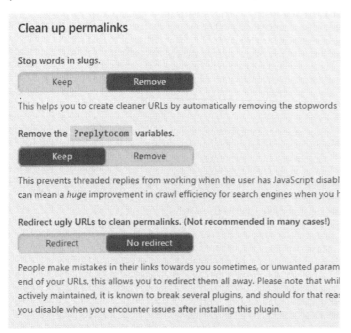

On the RSS tab, we have the option of inserting content into the RSS feeds:

An RSS feed is made up of a number of posts. These two boxes allow us to insert content before and after each post in the feed. You can leave these with the default settings. You can see that Yoast SEO automatically inserts a link back to your site. If you want specific things inserted before and after feed items, this is where you add them. The plugin offers you a few variables you can use.

That's it for the **Advanced** tab settings.

22.6. Tools

There are three tools included with this plugin. We won't go into detail, other than to summarize what they do.

The bulk editor allows you to save time with multiple title and description changes. Instead of having to go into the edit screen for each post and page, you can use this bulk edit tool. It looks like this:

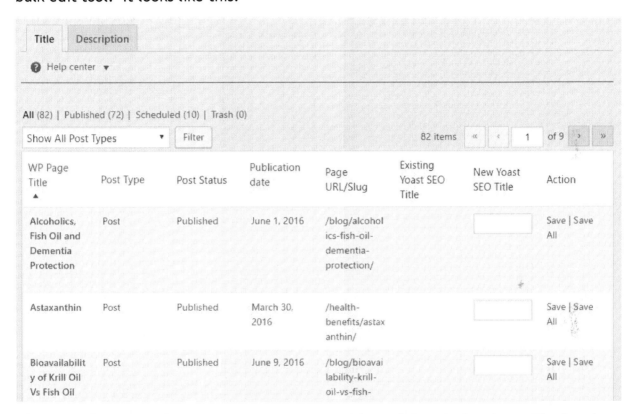

The two tabs across the top give you access to title and description data. The last but one column allows you to quickly type in a new "SEO Title" (and "SEO Description" on the description tab).

The file editor tool gives you quick access to two important files - the robots.txt and .htaccess. If you need to change these, you can do that here.

The import and export tools let you import and export settings from one SEO plugin to another, and from one website to another. We won't be looking at them here.

22.7. Search Console

The final menu in the SEO settings is the Search Console. Clicking on that takes you to a screen that allows you to connect the site to your Google Search Console account. If you followed the configuration wizard earlier, you'd have already done this. However, if you couldn't do it then (because you hadn't added your site to your GSC account), you can do it on this screen. Just click the **Get Google Authorization Code** button and follow the instructions.

OK, those are the global settings for Yoast's excellent SEO plugin. This plugin gives us tremendous power and control over the 'SEO settings' for our site, and the content it hosts.

The final part of this book shows how to set up another very important SEO plugin called **'W3 Total Cache'**. It helps to speed up the load times of your website, so is very useful. Let's take a closer look.

23. W3 Total Cache Setup

W3 Total Cache is one of several good WordPress caching plugins. If you are a WordPress veteran and have always used, and are happy with a different caching plugin, then I suggest you continue to use it.

If you have used W3 Total Cache before and know how to set it up, you can ignore this section.

Setting up W3 Total cache can be a little hit and miss sometimes, with some servers (or scripts on pages), disliking specific things you try to enable. It is, therefore, imperative that you make a backup of your database before you start to set up this plugin. The UpdraftPlus plugin mentioned earlier in the plugins section of this book is ideal for that.

I won't be covering all of the settings of this plugin. I will set you up with a good basic configuration, though, and one which should be compatible with most servers, templates, plugins and scripts. However, if you find your site has any problem loading, simply reverse the changes you made, or deactivate the plugin altogether.

OK, so before we look at how to set up this plugin, let's just cover the why again. Here are a couple of reasons *why* a caching plugin is a good idea.

1. In terms of SEO, the faster the site loads the better.

2. In terms of your visitor, no one likes to hang around waiting for your web page loads. If it takes too long (we're talking in seconds here), then they'll be hitting the back button and checking out your competitor sites instead.

23.1. Setting up W3 Total Cache

Before you start, I recommend you head over to GTMetrix.com and measure the speed of your site homepage. Here is mine:

Re-test a total of three times, and take an average of load times.

We'll now set up W3 Total Cache and retest.

I will assume you have already installed and activated the plugin since we covered that earlier.

In your WordPress Dashboard, you have a number of sub-menus under the **Performance** menu.

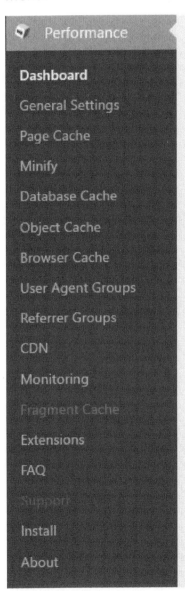

NOTE: I won't cover all of these settings, so just change the ones I do mention to the appropriate values. Assume that all other settings can be left at their default values.

23.1.1. General Settings

Click on the **General Settings** menu item.

This is where we can toggle the various caches on or off.

At the very top of the page, you have the option of toggling all caches on or off. You also have the option of enabling a **Preview Mode**. The preview mode will allow you to open up a preview window to see how the changes you've made are affecting your site before they go live. When you are happy with your settings, you can disable preview mode and save your settings. At that point, they will go live on your site.

If you want to use preview mode, that's fine. I am not going to bother.

Let's go and start enabling caches. Here are the settings.

Page Cache:

1. Enable page cache.

2. Page cache method – Disk enhanced.

Minify:

1. Enable minify.

2. Minify mode set to auto.

3. Minify cache method – Disk.

4. HTML minifier – Minify (default).

5. JS Minifier – JSMin (default).

6. CSS minifier – Minify (default).

Database Cache:

1. Enable database cache.

2. Database Cache Method – Disk

Object Cache:

1. Enable object cache.

2. Object cache method – Disk.

Browser cache:

1. Enable browser cache.

CDN:

Leave disabled for now. This is something you can activate and set up later, but you should contact your host support first, as some hosts, like StableHost, have easy integration with CDN. I use Stablehost and their free CDN and it made a big difference to the stability and speed of my site.

All other settings on the General Settings menu can be left at their default values.

Make sure you click the **Save Settings & Purge Caches** button before moving on.

Click on the **Page** Cache menu in the sidebar.

23.1.2. Page Cache

General:

These should all be disabled except:

1. Enable Cache posts page.

2. Enable Don't cache pages for logged in users.

Leave all other settings in the Page Cache at their default settings.

23.1.3. Minify

General:

1. Enable 'Rewrite URL structure'.

Leave these other settings at their default.

HTML & XML:

1. Enable HTML minify settings.

2. Check Inline CSS minification.

3. Check inline JS minification.

4. Check line break removal.

23.1.4. Browser Cache

General:

1. Enable 'Set last-modified header'.

2. Enable 'Set expires header'.

3. Enable 'Set cache control header'.

4. Enable 'Entity tag (eTag)'.

5. Enable 'W3 Total Cache header'.

6. Enable 'HTTP (gzip compression)'.

That's it! Your W3 Total Cache is now configured with conservative settings.

Using the Admin bar at the top of your website, select **Purge All Caches** from the **Performance** menu.

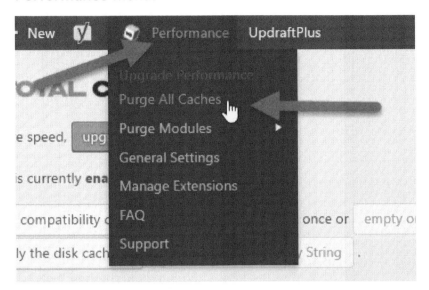

Now go back to GTMetrix.com and check your homepage speed. After the first check, re-test it a second time. The first time will take longer as the page won't be cached yet. The second run will give you a better idea of your true page load time.

As a reminder here was mine **BEFORE** installing W3 Total Cache:

And here is the same page **AFTER** W3 cache was installed and configured (these are the results on the second run after clearing the cache):

The homepage is now loading nearly two seconds quicker, with far fewer requests on the server. The total page size is down a little too. I'll probably check the images on this page to see if there are any large ones that need to be better optimized. The Smush Image Compressions and Optimization plugin could help with this.

That's it. Your Wordpress site is now highly optimized for the search engines and loads quickly. Congratulations!

Useful resources

All resources mentioned in this book can be found here:

http://ezseonews.com/wpseo

Please leave a review on Amazon

If you enjoyed this book, PLEASE leave a review on the Amazon website.

All the best

Andy Williams

My other Webmaster books

All of my books are available as Kindle books and paperbacks. You can view them all here:

http://amazon.com/author/drandrewwilliams

I'll leave you to explore those if you are interested. You'll find books on various aspects of being a webmaster such as creating high-quality content, SEO, CSS etc.

My Video Courses

I have a growing number of video courses hosted on Udemy. You can view a complete list of these at my site:

http://ezseonews.com/udemy

There are courses on the same kinds of topics that my books cover, so SEO, Content Creation, Wordpress, Website Analytics, etc.

More information from Dr. Andy Williams

If you would like more information, tips, tutorials or advice, consider signing up for my free weekly newsletter over at ezSEONews.com offering tips, tutorials, and advice to online marketers and webmasters. My newsletter, plus SEO articles, etc. will be delivered to your inbox. I cannot always promise a weekly schedule, but I do try ;)

Printed in Great Britain
by Amazon